Volunteerism in Geriatric Settings

Volunteerism in Geriatric Settings

Vera R. Jackson, DSW
Editor

Routledge
Taylor & Francis Group

LONDON AND NEW YORK

First published 1995 by The Haworth Press, Inc.

Published 2013 by Routledge
2 Park Square, Milton Park, Abingdon, Oxfordshire OX14 4RN
711 Third Avenue, New York, NY 10017, USA

First issued in paperback 2016

Routledge is an imprint of the Taylor & Francis Group, an informa business

Volunteerism in Geriatric Settings has also been published as *Activities Adaptation & Aging*, Volume 20, Number 1 1995.

Library of Congress Cataloging-in-Publication Data

Volunteerism in geriatric settings / Vera R. Jackson, editor,
    p. cm.
    Published also as v. 20, no. 1 of Activities, adaptation & aging.
    Includes bibliographical references and index.
    ISBN 978-1-315-82526-7 (eISBN)
    ISBN 978-1-56024-790-6

    1. Social work with the aged-United States. 2. Volunteer workers in social service-United States-Management. I. Jackson, Vera R.
HV1461.V65 1996
362.6'0973-dc20
    95-51301
    CIP

ISBN 13: 978-1-138-98685-5 (pbk)
ISBN 13: 978-1-56024-790-6 (hbk)

ABOUT THE EDITOR

Vera R. Jackson, DSW, ACSW, is the President of VEJAK Research & Management Services, an organization specializing in "Ethnogeriatrics," and a Research Scientist with the George Washington University. Dr. Jackson received a Bachelor of Arts degree in Psychology and Sociology from Trinity College, and Master of Social Work and Doctor of Social Work degrees from Howard University.

Dr. Jackson has an extensive research, program administration, and planning and evaluation background. She is the guest editor of a previous Haworth Press publication, *Aging Families and Use of Proverbs for Values Enrichment.*

Volunteerism in Geriatric Settings

CONTENTS

**Culinary Delights from Around the World
(International Cuisine Volunteer Program)**   **53**
Darlene J. Bruton

Gardening–An Equal Opportunity Joy   **71**
Pamela L. McKee

THE HOMELESS

CONCLUDING REMARKS

Foreword

Volunteerism has long been valued in America as a means of responding to the human resource needs of its citizenry. As our population becomes increasingly diverse, we find that government and other service organizations are under tremendous strain to provide for the array of needs that accompany this diverse population. Thus, as we continue to develop respect for individuals and strive to understand their needs, volunteerism takes on a heightened significance.

Kantrowitz (1989) suggests that after years of apathy, Americans are volunteering more than ever. A 1987-1988 survey by Independent Sector, an umbrella organization for most of the major charitable groups in the United States, reveals that 45% of the people surveyed volunteered regularly (Kantrowitz, 1989). This volunteer spirit is reported to cover an array of human needs in a variety of settings. Geriatric care facilities are a representative cluster of one such setting.

As Americans are living longer, the need for support services for the senior segment of the population becomes more acute. Much of the support needed comes from dedicated people giving of their time and talents to assist in the caring of seniors.

Volunteerism in Geriatric Settings is designed to help activity directors and other interested persons who work in geriatric settings plan and manage volunteer programs and broaden their understanding of what motivates people to volunteer. I commend Dr. Jackson for the scope of issues provided and their relevance to program vision and management.

Issues such as physical fitness, management styles of administrators of

---

[Haworth co-indexing entry note]: "Foreword." Redmond, Walter J. Jr. Co-published simultaneously in *Activities, Adaptation & Aging* (The Haworth Press, Inc.) Vol. 20, No. 1, 1995, pp. xvii-xviii; and: *Volunteerism in Geriatric Settings* (ed: Vera R. Jackson), The Haworth Press, Inc., 1995, pp. xv-xvi. Single or multiple copies of this article/chapter may be purchased from The Haworth Document Delivery Center [1-800-342-9678, 9:00 a.m. - 5:00 p.m. (EST)].

xv

senior care facilities, volunteer retention, gardening activities for nursing home residents, care of the homeless, and the spiritual needs of the elderly are addressed in this edition. Two particularly relevant issues also addressed are the linkages between the elderly and youths reflected in intergenerational programming and linkages between the elderly and international communities introduced through international culinary practices.

Volunteerism in Geriatric Settings exemplifies one significant means by which society may respond to the diverse needs of its aged.

Walter J. Redmond, Jr.
Assistant Professor, Sociology
University of the District of Columbia

REFERENCE

Kantrowitz, B. (1989). The new volunteers. *Newsweek*. pp. 36-38.

Acknowledgments

The editor would like to thank everyone who contributed to the development of this volume including the authors, telephone survey respondents, colleagues, and volunteers. A special and personal thanks is extended to her husband Wilbert and children, Brandon and Anjelica, for their love and support.

Thank you, God, for opening doors!

Introduction

Volunteer program management within geriatric settings requires a significant investment of time, commitment, and know-how. Extensive planning, professional development, creativity, resourcefulness, and an understanding of volunteer and resident needs are essential standards of operation. Moreover, program management requires the ability to compete for volunteers and to balance varied needs while avoiding frustration and burn-out.

The acknowledgment and appreciation of diversity within the field of volunteerism has necessitated the development of elaborate strategies designed to enhance program operations. Varied ethnic, religious, and socio-economic backgrounds are requiring the construction of new approaches and programs to enable volunteer managers to address equity issues. The significance of these issues can not be over-emphasized; clarity of resolve is central to the realistic setting of program goals and priorities.

A dimension of diversity that affects both volunteers and geriatric residents alike is related to programming. Many volunteers are now seeking programs that are unique in service content and that offer learning opportunities. Likewise, many geriatric residents want to learn from the programs offered and they seek occasions to volunteer to help others while also residing in these settings.

The recognition of differences among people and the need for creative programming and risk-taking will be the driving forces of volunteerism in the future whether we like it or not. Failure to prepare for these changes

---

[Haworth co-indexing entry note]: "Introduction." Jackson, Vera R. Co-published simultaneously in *Activities, Adaptation & Aging* (The Haworth Press, Inc.) Vol. 20, No. 1, 1995, pp. 1-2; and: *Volunteerism in Geriatric Settings* (ed: Vera R. Jackson), The Haworth Press, Inc., 1995, pp. 1-2. Single or multiple copies of this article/chapter may be purchased from The Haworth Document Delivery Center [1-800-342-9678, 9:00 a.m. - 5:00 p.m. (EST)].

1

will result in an ill prepared geriatric program that will be unable to compete with other settings for volunteers. The choice is up to each one of us to make a real investment in the future for our volunteer programs. Let us embrace this challenge with zeal, professionalism, and anticipation.

Vera R. Jackson, DSW, ACSW

UNDERSTANDING VOLUNTEERISM

The Nature of Caring in Volunteerism Within Geriatric Settings

Joseph Dancy, Jr.
M. Lorraine Wynn-Dancy

SUMMARY. Volunteerism within geriatric settings can enhance the emotional, social, and physical well-being of older adults. There are several salient features embodied in the act of caring. These include "levels of knowing," patience and courage which subsumes trust and hope. Intrinsic to the concept of genuine caring are the volunteer's abilities to empathize, empower, and engage the geriatric client. *[Article copies available from The Haworth Document Delivery Service: 1-800-342-9678.]*

INTRODUCTION

Numerous studies have pointed out that American society is "graying" as the number of persons age 65 and over is growing more rapidly than the rest of the population. "In fact the population age 85 and over is expected to more than triple in size between 1980 and 2030" (*Aging America*, 1991,

Joseph Dancy, Jr., PhD, is Gerontologist/Associate Professor in the Ethelyn R. Strong School of Social Work at Norfolk State University in Norfolk, VA. M. Lorraine Wynn-Dancy, MS, MA, is Assistant Professor and Program Director in the Department of Community Health and Rehabilitation at Norfolk State University in Norfolk, VA.

Address correspondence to the authors at: 1501 Hadley Court, Virginia Beach, VA 23456.

[Haworth co-indexing entry note]: "The Nature of Caring in Volunteerism Within Geriatric Settings." Dancy, Joesph Jr. and M. Lorraine Wynn-Dancy. Co-published simultaneously in *Activities, Adaptation & Aging* (The Haworth Press, Inc.) Vol. 20, No. 1, 1995, pp. 5-12; and: *Volunteerism in Geriatric Settings* (ed: Vera R. Jackson), The Haworth Press, Inc., 1995, pp. 5-12. Single or multiple copies of this article/chapter may be purchased from The Haworth Document Delivery Center [1-800-342-9678, 9:00 a.m. - 5:00 p.m. (EST)].

p. xix). This group, known as the "old-old," represents the fastest growing segment within the elderly population.

About five percent of the elderly live in institutional care settings, most of which are nursing home facilities (*Aging American,* 1991, p. xxiv). With the rapid increase in the numbers of older persons with social, financial, emotional, and especially health problems, there has been a rising demand for services, especially for the "old-old."

The older adult's life within the context of a geriatric setting is enhanced by volunteers who compensate for the often short-handed staff to provide the emotional, social and physical needs of elderly clients. Volunteers especially add to the health and wholeness of the older adult residents of geriatric settings when genuine caring is a vital dimension of volunteerism. In volunteerism the caring factor should be the undergirding bond in all that the volunteer does in relating to the older adult client or resident.

This article addresses the nature of caring in volunteerism within geriatric settings. The complexity of genuine caring is explored within a multifaceted framework which leads to the notion that genuine caring is, indeed, a spiritual act that leads a volunteer to action outside of dogma. But first of all, what is caring? How can genuine caring be described?

DEFINING THE CONCEPT OF CARING

Henri Nouwen, Milton Mayeroff and Nel Noddings have all given insight into the nature of caring. Nouwen has observed that "to care is to cry out with those who are ill, confused, lonely, isolated, and forgotten and to recognize their pain in our own hearts" (Nouwen, 1974, p. 34). Mayeroff extends the concept of caring by noting that "to care for another person, in the most significant sense, is to help him grow and actualize himself" (Mayeroff, 1971, p. 1). Still Noddings points toward the commitment to act as essential in genuine caring. She shares that "the commitment to act in behalf of the cared-for, –and the continued renewal of commitment over the appropriate span of time are the essential elements of caring from the inner view" (Noddings, 1984, p. 16). Thus, the above definitive aspects of caring suggest that intrinsic to the concept of caring is being able to *empathize,* to *empower* (enable), and to *engage* (act). This definitive understanding of caring provides saliency in the examination of caring in volunteerism within geriatric settings.

Certainly most directors of geriatric settings would generally readily agree with these definitions of the concept of caring. A person called a "good" volunteer is often described as a person who is committed and gives serious attention to those cared for.

In examining the concept of caring a distinction must be made between "caring about" versus "caring-for" another. The linguistic nuances suggest that to "care about" another implies cognitive reflection on the care of another. Noddings calls the notion of "caring about" others as maintaining "an internal state of readiness to try to care for whoever crosses our path" (Noddings, 1984, p. 18). This differs from "caring-for" another, and brings up the limitations of caring. Though the volunteer may "care about" many geriatric clients, he or she will be capable of genuine caring only with a designated and limited number.

What other limitations are subsumed within the concept of genuine caring? The volunteer within the geriatric setting risks being overwhelmed. There may be an abundance of client needs–physical, emotional and social–which beg for immediate attention. Indeed, Noddings comments:

> There exists in all caring situations the risk that the one-caring will be overwhelmed by the responsibilities and duties of the task and that, as a result of being burdened, he or she will cease to care for the other and become instead the object of "caring". (Noddings, 1984, p. 12)

Another limitation inherent in caring is vulnerability. Vulnerability means capable of being wounded. The volunteer within a geriatric setting who engages in genuine caring must risk the possibility of being scorned by the cared-for. In spite of the best efforts of the volunteer there may be times when the volunteer may be rejected by the cared-for resulting in the volunteer's hurt feelings. The person who engages in genuine caring must always be aware of this risk.

Since the concept of caring may have varying dimensions within different frameworks, it is important that training or orientation sessions for volunteers provide clarity about the nature of genuine caring, as well as its meaning and application within a particular setting. Such training then allows the volunteers to have the same level field of understanding about appropriate caring. Well-designed training also lifts the volunteers' consciousness to all aspects of genuine caring as well as removes the veil to reveal the limitations (e.g. vulnerability) inherent in the process of caring for the elderly.

SOME SALIENT FEATURES OF CARING FOR THE ELDERLY WITHIN GERIATRIC SETTINGS

Mayeroff (1971) has described caring as a developmental process with the relationship between the volunteer and the cared-for (the elderly) being constantly re-shaped through new insights within the process of knowing. "Knowing" can be defined as the act of understanding, having knowledge, information or insight (*Webster's Third New International Dictionary*, 1993, p. 1252).

The first level of "knowing" involves seeking to understand the elderly client by learning in general about the aging process, as well as the complexities, procedures and routines of the geriatric setting in which volunteer services are rendered. Thus, a fundamental question for those who provide the training for the volunteers is: What knowledge is required for volunteers to work effectively with the elderly in this particular setting? This knowledge base for the volunteers should, at least, include the psychological and physical aspects of aging (M. N. Ozawa, 1993, pp. 149-150). This first level of "knowing" allows the volunteer to eradicate inappropriate myths, stereotypes and fears about aging (Cox, Parsons, 1994, p. 8).

As the second level of "knowing" is approached, it is necessary to establish the fact that the average volunteer in a geriatric setting is providing care for a person or persons who were initially strangers. It is, therefore, imperative to explore the specific aspects of knowing and caring for the stranger.

Yet a third level of "knowing" is embodied within this salient feature of genuine caring. This is the level of the volunteer "knowing" self. The volunteer must be aware of what "luggage" he or she brings to the geriatric setting, for stored therein are values, attitudes, myths, beliefs and feelings that may or may not sharply contrast, or even clash, with those stored with the older adult. Difficult though it may be, it is necessary in "knowing" self to unpack one's "luggage" and examine the contents as objectively as possible so that those items in storage which would cause the volunteer to pass judgement or be less empathetic can be consciously left outside the geriatric setting.

Truly striving to know the senior adult is a major ingredient of empathy and promotes a strong bond between the volunteer and geriatric client. Certainly, the volunteer's attitude will reflect her/his understanding of the client. The volunteer's attitude also will affect the client's well-being:

> The one cared-for sees the concern, delight, or interest in the eyes of the one-caring and feels her warmth in both verbal and body language. To the cared-for no act in his behalf is quite as important or influential as the attitude of the one-caring. A major act done grudgingly may be accepted graciously on the surface but resented deeply inward, whereas a small act performed generously may be accepted nonchalantly but appreciated inwardly. When the attitude of the one-

caring bespeaks caring, the cared-for glows, grows stronger, and feels not so much that he has been given something as that something has been added to him. And this "something" may be hard to pacify. Indeed, for the one-caring and the cared-for in a relationship of genuine caring, there is no felt need on either part to specify what sort of transformation has taken place. (Noddings, 1989, pp. 19-20)

But how could a volunteer arrive at a sense of genuine knowing of a client in a geriatric setting without *patience?* Patience then is another salient feature of caring (M. Mayeroff, 1971). In a society where we are accustomed to speed and equating speed with efficiency the feature of patience becomes a challenge.

Patience implies not only providing the older adult with sufficient time to complete the necessary tasks, but the space to move toward self-actualization. It is empowering, enabling and affirming the elderly client to continue to grow at his or her own pace and providing the older adult the space to do so.

Not only must the volunteer develop patience with persons in geriatric settings, but the volunteer must develop patience with self. Mayeroff points out that the volunteer must give himself or herself time to really know and understand the cared-for, as well as to understand himself in that caring relationship. He observes that "I must give myself a chance to care" (Mayeroff, 1971, p. 19). Thus, the volunteer's movement toward engagement with the cared-for, as well as the cared-for's eventual empowerment are enhanced by patience within the genuinely caring relationship.

Another salient feature of caring is *courage*. The question could understandably be raised: Why does it take courage for the volunteer to genuinely care for the client in a geriatric setting? Mayeroff has cogitated that "the greater the sense of going into the unknown, the more courage is called for in caring" (Mayeroff, 1971, p. 28). A courageous volunteer has the capacity and willingness to share the unknown journey with the geriatric client in spite of the volunteer's own fears and uncertainty.

M. Scott Peck has expanded on Mayeroff's viewpoint by suggesting that "courage is the capacity to go ahead in spite of the fear, or in spite of the pain" (M. Scott Peck, 1993, p. 23). Indeed, the more the volunteer is willing to venture deeply into the unknown journey with the geriatric client, the more courage the volunteer will need to overcome his or her own anxieties and fears.

Certainly, a volunteer's sense of "knowing" self will be a distinctive yardstick in how well a volunteer charts unknown waters. There is risk involved, and the risk is not only related to the elderly person's often fragile health, but also there is the risk of, even at this juncture, the volunteer having the courage in caring to follow the appropriate lead of the cared-for. For even at this end point of life, there are yet new discoveries possible for both the cared-for and the one-caring. Indeed, it becomes too easy to settle into a comfortable routine of medicine-time, mealtime, rest time, etc. The courageous volunteer, though, remains ever ready for new insights and new knowledge that help the cared-for toward further growth.

Indeed, for the volunteer to invest self and time into an uncertain future and accompany the geriatric client where neither has ever gone before reflects the courage of caring. How does the volunteer find the necessary courage? Perhaps the anchoring of both trust and hope within the domain of courage provides the volunteer with essential fortitude. It certainly requires courage to trust and to hope. Thus, trust and hope might be said, then, to be embedded in courage (Mayeroff, 1971, pp. 25-28).

Alluding to trust brings one rather directly to *hope,* the other salient feature embedded in courage. The genuinely caring relationship between the volunteer and the geriatric client embodies hope. By engaging and involving the older adult, the caring volunteer seeks to empower the geriatric client to actualize whatever aspects of self he or she can.

Hooper (1994) has presented an innovative investigation of "hope behaviors" in clinicians in training which is germane to this discussion. In Hooper's study, hope behaviors clustered as follows: (1) listening skills, (2) leading skills, (3) reflecting skills, (4) summarizing skills, (5) confronting skills, (6) interpreting skills, and (7) informing skills. She observed that hope behaviors are "critical for patient progress, patient involvement in treatment, and cost effectiveness in clinical outcomes" (Hooper, 1994, p. 14).

The volunteer in a geriatric setting should emphasize a hope which values the possibilities of the present, and moves the geriatric client toward self-actualization. This hope is "an expression of the plentitude of the present, a present alive with a sense of the possible" (Mayeroff, 1971, p. 25).

An additional salient feature of caring is *humility.* The humility of the volunteer promotes the engagement and empowerment of the geriatric client. In a genuinely caring relationship humility embodies the idea that one can learn from the cared-for. It has been stated that "an attitude of not having anything further to learn is incompatible with caring" (Mayeroff, 1971, p. 23). Thus, the caring volunteer is "genuinely humble in being ready and willing to learn more about the other and himself, and what caring involves. This includes learning from the one cared for as well . . . " (Mayeroff, 1971, p. 23). Humility in caring incorporates the movement away from self (Noddings, 1984).

LISTENING AS A PROCESS FACTOR IN CARING

Hooper (1994) has observed that well-developed listening skills are a necessary adjunct to fostering hope behaviors within a geriatric setting. The volunteer needs careful training in the process of empathetic listening in order to build a genuinely caring relationship. Through training in listening the volunteer becomes ready to hear the geriatric client's story.

According to Hooper (1994) active listening involves these skills: (1) attending skills (careful listening and observing of both verbal and non-verbal messages), (2) Paraphrasing (restating the geriatric client's message to be sure it is understood), (3) Clarifying, self-disclosing and focusing discussion, and (4) Perception checking (determining the accuracy of what is heard).

CONCLUSION

Thus, the concept of caring embodies empathetic knowing which moves the cared-for to actualization or growth bolstered by the committed relationship with the volunteer within the geriatric setting. The commitment of the caring volunteer might be termed engrossment or engagement. The point being that a genuinely caring relationship is a focused relationship which empowers the cared-for.

Caring is viewed as a developmental process which allows the cared-for to continue to unfold. Salient features of a volunteer's positive caring relationship with a geriatric client include "knowing" or understanding the cared-for, patience, as well as courage which subsumes trust and hope. Finally, a genuinely caring relationship is marked by humility.

AUTHOR NOTE

Joseph Dancy, Jr. is a theologian/gerontologist. He received his undergraduate degree from Virginia Union University, and the Master of Divinity (M. Div.) degree from the School of Religion of Virginia Union University in Richmond, Virginia. He also earned the Master of Theology (Th.M.) degree from Princeton Theological Seminary in Princeton, New Jersey. He continued his education at the University of Michigan, Ann Arbor, Michigan, where he earned the Doctor of Philosophy (Ph.D.) degree in Educational Gerontology. He is the author of the book, *The Black Elderly: A Guide for Practitioners* and co-authored the books, *Mature/Older Job Seeker's Guide* and *Health Promotion for the Rural Black Elderly: A Program Planning and Implementation Guide.*

M. Lorraine Wynn-Dancy received her undergraduate degree from Hampton

University, a Master's degree (M.S.) in Speech and Hearing Science from Michigan State University and a Master's degree (M.A.) in Linguistics from The University of Michigan, Ann Arbor, Michigan. She has completed additional studies at the University of Nigeria, in Nussuka, Nigeria, West Africa and at Stanford University in Palo Alto, California.

REFERENCES

Butler, R. (1975). *Why Survive? Being Old in America.* New York: Harper & Row Publishers.

Cox, E. O., Parsons, R. J. (1994). "Empowerment-Oriented Social Work, Practice with the Elderly." Pacific Grove, CA: Brooks/Cole Publishers.

Goodman, C. C. (1984). Helper Bank: "A Reciprocal Services Program for Older Adults." *Social Work,* July-August, pp. 397-398.

Hooper, Celia. "The Modeling And Assessment of 'Hope Behaviors' in speech-language Pathology Graduate Students." American Speech-Language-Hearing Association's Administration and Supervision Special Interest Division Newsletter. Vol. 4. No.3. November, 1994, pp. 13-17.

Hooyman, N. R., Kiyak, H. S. (1988). *Social Gerontology.* Boston: Allyn & Bacon Company.

Kerschner, H. K. and Butler, F. F. (1994). "Productive Aging and Senior Volunteerism: Is the U. S. Experience Relevant?" In R. R. Enright, Jr., (Ed.), *Perspectives in Social Gerontology.* Boston: Allyn & Bacon Company.

Mayeroff, M. (1971). *On Caring.* New York: Perennial Library, Harper & Row Publishers.

Noddings, N. (1984). *Caring.* Berkeley: University of California Press.

Nouwen, H. J. M. (1975). *Reaching Out.* Garden City, New York: Doubleday Company.

Nouwen, H. J. M. (1974). *Out of Solitude.* Notre Dame, Indiana: Ave Maria Press.

Nouwen, H. J. M. (1972). *The Wounded Healer.* Garden City, New York: Doubleday Company.

Ozawa, M. N., Howell-Marrow, N. (1993). "Missouri Service Credit System for Respite Care: An Exploratory Study." *Journal of Gerontological Social Work.* Vol. 21 (1/2), pp. 147-160. New York: The Haworth Press, Inc.

Peck, M. S. (1993). *Further Along the Road Less Traveled.*New York: Simon and Schuster Publisher.

Thurman, H. (1963). *Disciplines of the Spirit.* Richmond, Indiana: Friends United Press.

Tournier, P. (1984). *A Listening Ear.* Minneapolis: Augsburg Publisher.

U. S. Senate Special Committee on Aging. (1991). *Aging America: Trends and Projections.* Washington, D. C.

Webster's Third New International Dictionary. (1993).

PLANNING

Finding Nursing Home Volunteers
with Staying Power

Melissa H. Duncan

SUMMARY. Finding quality volunteers is never an easy task and keeping them is even more difficult. I have built a thriving volunteer program by critically reviewing and restructuring the basic foundation. I have developed an efficient and comprehensive training program that emphasizes effective communication on all levels. My training technique emphasizes role playing and educating the volunteer about validation. This hands-on technique is enthusiastically received by volunteers, is practical and produces good results. *[Article copies available from The Haworth Document Delivery Service: 1-800-342-9678.]*

It has been my experience that perhaps the most common mistake made when soliciting volunteers is approaching the task from a "me" point of view. The "what's in it for us" attitude can be one of the greatest stumbling blocks one experiences when trying to create a quality volunteer program. My volunteer program has experienced increasingly measurable success when it was restructured to consider the needs of the volunteers first. Ask yourself how the facility and residents can be of benefit to those offering their valuable time, and the recruitment process takes on a whole new flavor. Examine the motivational reasons behind volunteerism and adapt your program accordingly. After all, the average nursing home resi-

Melissa H. Duncan, C.T.R.S., is Director of Recreational Therapy, Volunteer Services and Corporate Consultant for Medlantic Long Term Care.

Address correspondence to the author at: 4373 Lee Highway, Unit #408, Arlington, VA 22207.

[Haworth co-indexing entry note]: "Finding Nursing Home Volunteers With Staying Power." Duncan, Melissa H. Co-published simultaneously in *Activities, Adaptation & Aging* (The Haworth Press, Inc.) Vol. 20, No. 1, 1995, pp. 15-23; and: *Volunteerism in Geriatric Settings* (ed: Vera R. Jackson), The Haworth Press, Inc., 1995, pp. 15-23. Single or multiple copies of this article/chapter may be purchased from The Haworth Document Delivery Center [1-800-342-9678, 9:00 a.m. - 5:00 p.m. (EST)].

15

dent has so many needs that I can not imagine that the talents and strengths any individual volunteer has to offer can not be utilized in an effective manner.

ASSESSMENT OF THE VOLUNTEER

As a trained recreational therapist I spend a great deal of my time making clinical assessments of clientele. I have used those same techniques when interviewing individual potential volunteers and volunteer groups. Initially, I examine why the volunteer has sought out my nursing home. There are as many reasons why people volunteer as there are volunteers. It is much easier to match up a volunteer's unique talents with a task when one has determined the motivation behind the offer to perform work for no compensation.

Secondly, I try to make a brief demographic analysis of the potential volunteer or group of volunteers. It only stands to reason that I am not going to expect a group of junior high students to perform duties with the same level of maturity as a group of college educated gerontologists. I also pay close attention to the backgrounds of the volunteers in correlation to my resident population. Do they have numerous things in common or do they hail from vastly different backgrounds? Demographics can play a big role in determining the potential effectiveness in communication between the volunteer and the geriatric.

Perhaps the most critical aspect of volunteer assessment is determining the strengths of the individual while also acknowledging his or her personal limitations. It can be program sabotage to place a volunteer in a position for which he or she is unqualified, ill-prepared or feels awkward. Talk to your volunteers. Find out something about them as people. Practice effective listening skills when questions are asked of you. Capitalize on those strengths and respect the limitations. Be realistic: the shy or quiet volunteer is not the perfect choice to lead a group but that same individual may flourish in a one-on-one setting. A spiritually strong volunteer can perhaps be easily motivated to design and implement a bible study group but may fail miserably when asked to teach crafts or assist with the exercise hour. I can not over stress–MATCH THE TALENT WITH THE TASK AT HAND.

Assessment of volunteers must be an ongoing process. As one is exposed to the non-paid staff, a clearer picture of the individuals is established. Don't allow yourself to become inflexible with regards to volunteer assignments. Adaptation is the cornerstone of any good volunteer program. You must be able to determine the level of reinforcement required to keep individuals happy and productive.

As a manager of people, it is crucial to be fair. However, that does not require that everything be equal. Just as we adapt programs and volunteer opportunities to allow the individual volunteer's talents to be highlighted, we must alter the form and amount of reinforcement to reflect the individual's need for said reinforcement. Some volunteers require consistent positive reinforcement from the facility staff, whereas others may feel completely satisfied by the appreciation shown by actual residents. The fiercely independent volunteer may find constant positive strokes from staff as intrusive while another volunteer may need to hear he or she is needed and appreciated during each visit to the facility.

Approaching volunteerism from the perspective of what the facility can do for the volunteer, endows your program with opportunities for success. Volunteers who sense their role is vital to the operation of the nursing home and the well-being of the resident population will become very loyal to the organization. The individuals who are comfortable in their roles, while also feeling appreciated, generally place their volunteer obligations as a top priority in their lives. Create a loyal volunteer population and the big winners will be the geriatric residents.

FAMILIARIZING THE VOLUNTEERS
WITH THE POPULATION SERVED

A key factor in creating a comfortable environment for the volunteer is educating them about what they can expect to see. For centuries man has been afraid of the unknown and for many volunteers nursing home life is uncharted waters. To complicate the issue many persons have strongly defined preconceived ideas about what life in a nursing home is like and generally, those ideas are saturated in negativity. So how do you, as the professional, turn that around?

It is crucial for you to appreciate the fact that in American society, getting old is nothing to aspire to. Geriatrics are typically not a very appealing population with which one may wish to work. For most Americans OLD equals LOSS: loss of independence, loss of cognitive acuity, loss of physical prowess, loss of dignity, loss of respect and an overall loss of one's ability to function adequately in today's society. I have found it is best to be very candid about these things. When orienting the new volunteer remind him or her that a nursing home is not just a retirement community but rather, a health care facility. Persons residing in a nursing home are there for a reason. Every geriatric placed in a home has some deficit, whether it is immediately apparent or not. That deficit may be a physical or medical problem. It may be related to emotional instability or cognitive loss but, the severity is always such that around the clock long term care nursing is required. Making the volunteer keenly aware of the fact that every person in the home needs to be there can be instrumental in educating the volunteer to the high level of patience needed when interacting with the elderly.

One of the easiest and most effective ways to prepare volunteers and to assure that they will provide quality service is to share basic demographic information about the residents with the volunteers. Just as demographics helps you to assess the qualities of the volunteers, it can provide the volunteers with some very helpful information. For effective communication to occur we must establish a common ground for the actual interaction. A person can learn a great deal about how they should communicate by knowing something of one's basic background. Instinctively, one knows one must adapt the conversation format when speaking to residents who are primarily frail, poor, uneducated, and were limited by geographic and racial constraints all their lives in comparison to how one may approach a group of elderly, retired, military generals who have their cognitive capabilities fully intact.

At this point it is helpful to educate the volunteers about some of the common physical aspects that accompany the aging process. A prime example being . . . volunteers need to know that as we age, four of our five senses tend to deteriorate at a significant rate. Only touch develops a heightened level of sensitivity with age. This can be very useful information for a novice volunteer. This little bit of information can be translated into a clear message for the volunteer. It says, "don't be afraid to touch these people and if you want to get your message across you may have to tap into as many of the elderly person's senses as realistically possible." We want the volunteer experience to be positive for the volunteer as well as the older person. Taking steps to assure that communication is effective can only help to make interactions fulfilling for all concerned.

It can also be very useful to new volunteers to know that the response of the elderly patient to a given disease may be quantitatively different to the response a young adult may have to the exact same disorder. Those unfamiliar with geriatric populations do not fully appreciate the aged person who is declining physically and extremely vulnerable to any ill health development. Volunteers need to be aware that by coming into the geriatric setting with a simple head cold, they may be placing an older person in grave physical danger. It is also helpful for volunteers to be aware that many older persons experience a temporary but notable difference in mental alertness when ill.

If possible, it is nice during orientation to be able to give new recruits not only an overall picture of the aging process, but to clue them into medical issues which are specifically prevalent in your facility. This is also a perfect time to make them aware of certain facility procedures regarding the identification of residents with special medical needs. Your institution may use color coded identification bracelets or pictorial door signs to alert others to the health concerns of the patients. The more information the volunteer has going into the geriatric setting the better prepared they will be when unusual circumstances arise. The amount of ease demonstrated by the volunteers with regards to their role and purpose is in direct proportion to the level of knowledge and education they have received about their jobs and the elderly.

TRICKS TO MAKING THE EDUCATION PROCESS FAST AND EFFECTIVE

Let's face it, you want to get your biggest bang for your buck when training and orienting new recruits. This is where those assessments of the volunteers becomes extremely useful. Obviously, one is not going to spend a great deal of time orienting volunteers who are making a "one-shot" appearance at the nursing home. These folks get the "10 minute special" about basic safety, resident rights, communication technique hints and the objectives of the day. The very best you can hope for perhaps is that you were entertaining enough to stimulate some interest and one or two persons out of the group will return for a second chance at volunteerism. The people who deserve more of your time and energy are those who have made a commitment to come to the Home on a regular basis.

So what is the best way to reach these people? For the education process to be effective it must be engaging and unlike school. Keep in mind that your main objective is the effective dissemination of information while creating an environment which is comfortable, yet conducive to learning. I have found ROLE PLAYING to be a very effective tool to accomplish said task. It actively involves the volunteer right from the start. The hands-on approach can produce learning that is highly effective while often being entertaining as well.

The real benefit to role playing is that the volunteer gets first hand insight of what to expect and what is expected of him. Role playing is the trial run to the real thing. It is the one place in which mistakes are welcomed because making them provides us with an ideal avenue by which to learn. There is a lot of security in knowing that a mistake made during this time will not negatively impact the elderly patient. Role playing also provides the volunteer an opportunity to show off his or her stuff. We like to be recognized for our positive traits and talents, and the role play environment is a perfect place to openly express those skills.

Finally, role playing lends itself perfectly to being able to make a demonstrative statement about one's personal or professional credibility. While the volunteer is displaying his hidden talents and intrinsic worthiness, you can acquaint the volunteer with your high level of expertise in the area of geriatrics. This may in fact demonstrate to the new recruit that you are someone who can be depended upon. Seize this opportunity as a time of building a trusting relationship with your volunteer.

EFFECTIVE COMMUNICATION

As long as two or more people inhabit the earth, there will be discussion about effective communication. And as long as theoreticians remain in this world, effective communication techniques will always be a hot topic of debate.

The subject of nursing homes and volunteers can not be honestly deliberated unless an evaluation of communication is included. As a volunteer manager you are responsible for communication on many different levels. You must monitor the communication that occurs between the nursing home residents and the volunteers, the staff and the volunteers, the volunteers amongst themselves and finally, your own ability to effectively interface with your volunteers. Our first priority, however, must be the residents and their opportunity to effectively communicate with the volunteer population.

As discussed briefly earlier, there are several tips you can share with your volunteers to assist them in getting the "physical" message across to the elderly patient. Effective use of touch, maximizing sensory stimulation, body positioning, establishing eye contact prior to conversation, speaking with clarity and adequate (but not obtrusive) volume are all simple basic instructions that you should share with the novice volunteer. I would like to examine, however, in greater detail, some of the psychological bases of communication with the elderly.

It is absolutely necessary to help the volunteer recognize the importance of meeting the resident on his own level. It is basic human nature that one does not appreciate being talked down to, figuratively or literally. It is a simple task to warn the new volunteer about not towering over an elderly person when speaking. It is a slightly more difficult task to convey to the volunteer the importance of respecting the person and his abilities when verbally interacting. Growing old and even losing some of one's cognitive acuity does not dictate that one should now be addressed in a child-like manner. Geriatrics are adults and should be treated as such. This is where "role playing training" can be an extremely effective tool in demonstrating how to and how not to carry on a conversation with an older person.

Reminding the volunteer that it is his or her job to formulate some opinion about the communication capabilities of any one particular resident is essential. The volunteer runs a great risk of showing disrespect to the elderly person if they are trying to maintain a level of interaction that the aged person no longer has the physical capability to perform. It can be quite demoralizing to the resident. Regardless of whether a person has highly developed verbalization skills or an extreme deficit such as aphasia, there are means to communicate effectively and with dignity.

I have found one of the biggest gifts I have given my volunteers in the training process is to educate them about validating a resident during interactions. I break the concept of validation therapy down to simple and easy to understand terms for my volunteers. I instruct volunteers to respond to the residents in a fashion which clearly indicates that they were listening or are sensitive to the emotional message or tone of the communication. This is not a license to buy into every fantasy a resident may have but rather, is a simple reaffirmation to the person that what he or she had to say was important. You are saying to that geriatric, "You count, you are worthy of my attention."

I fear one of the greatest injustices we show towards our elderly, especially those persons residing in a nursing home, is that we have stopped listening. We all like to be listened to when we speak and growing old does not diminish that desire. This is a very easy concept to convey in the training of volunteers. For example, when a confused resident begins to talk about the fact that she went to third grade together with a volunteer (and the volunteer is fairly certain that this is an inaccurate statement), the volunteer's response could be, "Boy, I loved third grade. What was your favorite thing about elementary school?" This response precisely declares to the elderly woman that the volunteer was listening to what she was talking about without being dishonest in response.

Another way in which one can validate a person is simply by showing sensitivity to his or her present emotional state. This can also be easily demonstrated in a teaching example. I may ask my middle school volunteers to imagine how sad and angry they would be if they just arrived home after not making the last cut to the basketball team and getting a C+

on their science project which they spent weeks doing. Then I ask them how they would react to their mother coming in their room and babbling away about what a beautiful day it is and how great it is to be alive. The general response is the typical student would NOT care to hear at all about how wonderful life is and most of them would prefer to sulk or be left alone. I then ask the students to apply this same response to our residents. The message is–if you find a resident who is exuberant, go ahead and join them in his or her enthusiasm. Conversely, if you come upon a resident who is sad and tearful, this is the time to show some gentle tenderness and concern and not the time to be acting like the vivacious Rebecca of Sunnybrook Farm. The simple training lesson here is to approach the residents with some sensitivity, meeting them where they are emotionally and not where you wish they were, or where you think they should be.

With regards to communication between the volunteers themselves and with the staff, the best advice I have is be a watchdog. You must be the one who monitors the activity of your volunteers to assure things are running smoothly. You must assume the role of mediator if necessary. You must make judgments about the role and placement of volunteers if the situation observed is disruptive to the smooth functioning of the facility.

Perhaps the easiest way to keep a handle on the daily functions of your volunteer staff is to create an environment in which they feel they can come to you with any problem which may arise in the Home. It is vital that you convey to the volunteers that you expect mistakes to be made. Accidents will happen, conflicts may arise but, unless the volunteer feels comfortable to come to you about these possible problems you are not going to be able to address or resolve them. You must work hard to maintain an approachable image. The safety and welfare of your residents is reliant upon that fact.

CONCLUSION

I need to emphasize that extensive education, assessments, lengthy training, and high quality of volunteer recruitment may be all for not if you ignore the "fun factor" in the volunteer experience. If the volunteer assignments feel too much like work your volunteers will resign as quickly as they have signed up. You can never lose sight of the fact that this is work for which there is no monetary compensation. The rewards must be intrinsic because by the definition of "volunteerism" the rewards may not be extrinsic. It is your obligation, as the professional, to create those opportunities for intrinsic compensation.

It is especially important to captivate the attention of the volunteer, as well as the attention of the geriatric when organizing intergenerational activities involving younger children. For example, as a recreational therapist, I work hard to plan the "fun" or high energy activities around my youth volunteers. You must recognize your volunteers take their cues from you, as do the residents. When I am orienting volunteers I become the poster child for pep and enthusiasm. It is extremely beneficial to carry that enthusiasm over in your introductions of the volunteers to the resident population. You want the residents to sense that the mere presence of these volunteers is something very special and in fact, it can be. Take a personal interest in your volunteers. If Zeke, the volunteer, does not show up one afternoon and normally you can set your watch by him, give him a call. Find out if he is okay.

You would be surprised of the mileage you can gain from having a yearly wiener roast to show your appreciation for your volunteers or by taking the time to send out holiday greeting cards. When possible, I also offer my established volunteers continued in-service training. Often they can benefit from an in-service that is being offered for the staff, family members or possibly a training session geared towards the volunteer. The more you can give, the more you will get. This just reinforces the concept of determining what you and the facility can do for the volunteer.

The lives of your resident population can be deeply enriched by the presence of volunteers especially for those residents who do not have outside support from family or persons they knew prior to admission. The relationships residents develop with the volunteers can become primary and prominent. The quality of in-house programs, especially recreation programs, is generally vastly enhanced by volunteers.

Whether or not volunteers are an asset to your nursing home is your ultimate responsibility. It is a responsibility which deserves serious consideration.

AUTHOR NOTE

Melissa H. Duncan, CTRS, received her Bachelor of Science degree from the University of Wyoming. Ms. Duncan has been employed as a recreation professional for more than 16 years, 14 of those years were spent working with special populations (retarded persons and geriatrics). Ms. Duncan maintains memberships with the American Therapeutic Recreation Association and the Bio-Ethics Network of Washington.

ADMINISTRATION

Management Styles That Can Help or Hurt Your Volunteer Program

Vera R. Jackson

SUMMARY. Activity director interviews offer a glimpse of the management styles most often observed in nursing homes. After a self-evaluation exercise, activity directors receive a strategy for the enrichment of their volunteer programs. *[Article copies available from The Haworth Document Delivery Service: 1-800-342-9678.]*

THE ISSUE

Much attention has been given to the recruitment, training, and recognition of volunteers working in a number of geriatric settings. Yet, one rarely discussed topic in this proliferation of information is the management style of the person with oversight responsibility for said programs.

The vision for the implementation of many volunteer programs is often dictated by a number of entities: senior management, staff, residents, residents' families, funding sources, and regulatory groups. However, once evolved, the volunteer program becomes one of many other services offered by the geriatric facility and must be directed as such, generally by one individual.

Vera R. Jackson, DSW, ACSW, is President of VEJAK Research & Management Services, Executive Director of a non-profit agency, and Research Scientist with The George Washington University.

Address correspondence to the author at: 5808 Westbrook Drive, New Carrollton, MD, 20784.

[Haworth co-indexing entry note]: "Management Styles That Can Help or Hurt Your Volunteer Program," Jackson, Vera R. Co-published simultaneously in *Activities, Adaptation & Aging* (The Haworth Press, Inc.) Vol. 20, No. 1, 1995, pp. 27-32; and: *Volunteerism in Geriatric Settings* (ed: Vera R. Jackson), The Haworth Press, Inc., 1995, pp. 27-32. Single or multiple copies of this article/chapter may be purchased from The Haworth Document Delivery Center [1-800-342-9678, 9:00 a.m. - 5:00 p.m. (EST)].

27

The direction or management of volunteer programs has, as a rule, varied according to facility, staffing, clientele, and geographical area. In many geriatric settings, the activity director has long held the responsibility for the operation of volunteer programs.

An activity director is often charged with finding creative ways of keeping many balls in the air, including the satisfaction balls of his/her supervisor, co-workers, residents, residents' families, and external groups. Moreover, the activity director must be willing to incorporate the geriatric setting's needs, organizational culture, and their own personality and style into volunteer program operations.

This discussion will focus upon the management styles of activity directors and the corresponding impact upon volunteer programs. The goals of this examination are self-discovery and self-evaluative in purpose. They are intended to: (1) enable activity directors to peer through a "looking glass" to determine if their management style is conducive to getting the best out of their volunteers; and, (2) afford activity directors information that will allow them to make the necessary adjustments towards establishing a successful volunteer program.

THE PROCESS

A telephone survey was developed to capture the management style of activity directors. The interview consisted of the following open-ended questions:

- Consider for a moment the volunteer programs that operate in geriatric settings. In general terms, describe the interaction between the person with the management responsibility for the program and the volunteers.
- Describe the manager's style including characteristics, traits, attitudes, and behavior.
- Describe your most favored management style. Why?
- Describe your least favored management style. Why?

Fifty-seven activity directors (or their counterparts) employed in nursing homes within Region III (Delaware, Pennsylvania, Virginia, West Virginia, Maryland, and the District of Columbia) participated in the study. The sample was randomly selected from the American Association of Homes and Services for the Aging's *Directory of Members* (1995).

Telephone interviews yielded information regarding the existence of three very distinct volunteer management styles that seem to operate within geriatric settings. These management styles appear to be more or less pronounced according to respondent interviews.

The proceeding management styles, which are a compilation of respondent interviews, have been categorized and labelled for presentation. This discussion will begin with a description of the management style deemed the least positive by respondents and will progress from there.

Discordant Management

"Discordant Management" is often thought to be the "worst of the worst" management style. The Discordant Manager does not want to operate a volunteer program. They would actually rather do everything themselves or with the support of paid staff. They often hate their jobs. Volunteers are a big inconvenience.

The Discordant Manager dislikes or distrusts their volunteers. These managers often accuse their volunteers of lacking relevant skills and experience; being unreliable; requiring excessive supervision; and encroaching on job security (Ilsley, 1990; Brudney, 1990).

Discordant Managers often derive pleasure in berating their volunteers and they operate in a manner that suggests to all that their volunteers are incompetent. The sentiment exists that volunteers should be kept at a distance because the more they know, the more likely they are to usurp the volunteer manager's authority. To guard against this probability, the Discordant Manager will spend tremendous amounts of time establishing rigid operational and supervisory protocols so as to limit the volunteer's ability to contribute in any viable fashion.

Ambivalent Management

"Ambivalent Managers," on the other hand, tolerate their volunteers because they know that "senior management" or external entities expect them to do so. Unlike the Discordant Manager described in the previous section, Ambivalent Managers neither like nor dislike their volunteers. In this instance, the volunteer is usually left alone as long as they "don't get in anybody's way." Only when a problem arises is a prudent plan of action instituted which usually consists of some moderate supervision for volunteers or the volunteers' engagement in program planning– just until things quiet down.

The Ambivalent Manager is typically the person who embraces their volunteers or program when it is convenient for them. These managers often maintain a log of volunteers they can call on for high visibility "special projects," but fail to find creative ways of incorporating any of these "special projects" into the very fabric of the geriatric volunteer program.

Ambivalent Managers attend training sessions and seminars for professional development purposes, but they fail to implement strategies learned. These managers often see no future for themselves in their current job.

Concordant Management

"Concordant Managers" love their volunteers. They often seek ways of show-casing volunteers and are pleased with the contributions. Concordant Managers look for creative ways of enhancing services with volunteer input.

Volunteers are often given the opportunity for advancement in the geriatric setting's volunteer hierarchy and performance evaluations are used as a means of allowing volunteers to excel and grow in their jobs. The volunteer program is structured and is generally reviewed annually. There is usually a high demand for volunteer assignments and sometimes a waiting list of volunteers eager to work for the organization.

Concordant Managers really enjoy their jobs. They are active in their professional associations and look for opportunities to network with their peers. Some managers find ways of grooming their volunteers for upcoming paid staff positions in the department.

The recognition of volunteers is a high priority. Many Concordant Managers are past or present volunteers who can fully appreciate the need for a well structured volunteer program that incorporates volunteer input.

REALITY CHECK

If you find yourself looking into a mirror and gazing into the eyes of the Discordant or Ambivalent Management style, don't fret or fear, there is hope for you. While admitting you have a problem in your management style is the first step towards a solution, you still have a significant amount of work to do. Instead of "blaming the victim" (a.k.a. volunteer), let's consider a plan of action that can change your management style from the least favored to the most favored.

PLAN OF ACTION

1. Identify those elements of your job that you find the most enjoyable. Likewise, list those elements that are the most painful to accomplish.
2. On 3 × 5 index cards write one element of your job that you find enjoyable. In very visible areas of your office, post these index cards as reminders of those things you like and find the most motivating.
3. Review the management styles outlined earlier and determine what traits and characteristics match your management traits and characteristics.
4. Compile a list of the most painful elements of your job along with your management traits and characteristics. Divide this list into two columns: "Things I Can Change" and "Things I Can Not Change."
5. Seek out an activity director that has a Concordant Management Style. Ask them to serve as a mentor for you as you attempt to develop reasonable time frames and solutions for your "Things I Can Change" list.
6. Seek out feedback on your program from volunteers. Organize focus groups and charge the groups with the development of strategies for enhancing your volunteer program.
8. Implement suggestions from the focus group sessions that are reasonable and within your sphere of responsibility.
9. Attend workshops and seminars that offer professional development in the area of volunteer administration.
10. Join professional associations and meet informally with local Activity Directors at least monthly.
11. Routinely evaluate your progress and make adjustments as needed.
12. Recognize your strengths and seek opportunities to promote those things you do well.

CONCLUSION

Managerial styles are based partly on the needs of the organization and partly on the activity director's personality. Some activity directors dislike volunteers and are threatened by their very existence; others like and trust volunteers and perceive them as "pure gold." Each of these attitudes, including the corresponding beliefs and values, will certainly impact the administration of the volunteer program.

Some of you may need a career change. Some of you many need to find a support group that can assist you in making needed changes or in accepting those things you can not change. Others may need to implement an innovative program or fresh approach to allow the "creative and motivational juices" to flow again. If you are in the latter group, the collection of innovative programs and approaches in this journal may be what you need to breathe new life into your program.

AUTHOR NOTE

Dr. Jackson received a Bachelor of Arts degree in Psychology and Sociology from Trinity College and both the Master of Social Work and Doctor of Social Work degrees from Howard University.

Dr. Jackson is a member of the National Association of Social Workers and the Greater Washington Society of Association Executives. She maintains membership on several boards and civic organizations.

Dr. Jackson has developed strategic plans for practitioners, educators, and researchers in the area of volunteer program development within geriatric settings. She has also written articles, books, and manuals on aging family proverbs, depression and aging, mental health planning in nursing homes, religiosity and spiritually, financing assistive technology, chronic illness, and death and dying.

REFERENCES

Brudney, J.L. (1990). *Fostering Volunteer Programs in the Public Sector: Planning, Initiating and Managing Volunteer Activities*. San Francisco: Jossey-Bass Publishers.

Directory of Members. (1995). American Association of Homes and Services for the Aging. Washington, D.C.

Ilsley, P. J. (1990). *Enhancing the Volunteer Experience: New Insights on Strengthening Volunteer Participation, Learning, and Commitment*. San Francisco: Jossey-Bass Publishers.

Morrison, E. K. (1988). *Working with Volunteers: Skills for Leadership*. Tucson, Arizona: Fisher Books.

CREATIVE PROGRAMMING

Volunteers of the Spirit:
Quality of Life Programming
with Religious Volunteers

Janet Grenon Ragno .

SUMMARY. Adjustment to the nursing home is a difficult task for the new resident. The loss of familiar surroundings, friends, health or absence from loved ones can disorient and cause physical and behavioral manifestations during the adjustment period. Community support from religious volunteers can renew a sense of well-being, purpose, belonging and solace through a variety of appropriate spiritual and religious activities. Participation in these events support not only the residents but their families, friends, and nursing home staff. *[Article copies available from The Haworth Document Delivery Service: 1-800-342-9678.]*

The variety of residents in a nursing home setting challenge the professional activity director's ability to provide a "Quality of Life Program"

Janet Grenon Ragno, ADC, is Activity Director and Social Service Designee at the Althea Woodland Nursing Home.

Address correspondence to the author at: Althea Woodland Nursing Home, 1000 Daleview Drive, Silver Spring, MD 20906.

[Haworth co-indexing entry note]: "Volunteers of the Spirit: Quality of Life Programming with Religious Volunteers." Ragno, Janet Grenon. Co-published simultaneously in *Activities, Adaptation & Aging* (The Haworth Press, Inc.) Vol. 20, No. 1, 1995, pp. 35-39; and: *Volunteerism in Geriatric Settings* (ed: Vera R. Jackson), The Haworth Press, Inc., 1995, pp. 35-39. Single or multiple copies of this article/chapter may be purchased from The Haworth Document Delivery Center [1-800-342-9678, 9:00 a.m. - 5:00 p.m. (EST)].

containing the three elements of empowerment, maintenance and support that OBRA regulations mandate (*Federal Register*, 1991). A careful assessment of each resident must be made to ascertain their activity and social interests to insure their well-being.

One area that needs particular scrutiny is religious affiliation. Family members, friends, ministers, other interested persons and the residents themselves can share important insights about the residents' spiritual and religious life. On assessment, it may be determined that the new resident had been very active in their religious community before they broke their hip. Perhaps they were elders in their church or led Bible studies. Another resident may have watched the Mass for Shut-Ins each Sunday morning. Hospice residents may have "unfinished business," wish to "make peace with their Maker" or make a life review before they die (Kalina, 1993). The interdisciplinary staff needs to actively listen to each resident and observe them for withdrawal, refusal to eat or negative comments about themselves as a symptom of unmet spiritual, as well as physical or social needs.

A comprehensive interdenominational religious volunteer program is instrumental in maintaining a quality of life program for those with demonstrated spiritual needs. Many different denominations are represented at the Althea Woodland Nursing Home and they serve our residents, families, and staff in a variety of ways.

DIFFERENT DENOMINATIONS

The Church of Christ visits our residents on the first and fifth Sundays of the month. There is an announcement at their service that they will be visiting the Althea Woodland and that all are invited to attend. Several families and the minister, Ted Thomas, hold a prayer service full of readings and familiar songs.

The atmosphere promotes a sense of belonging and acceptance especially with the presence of young parents with their children. The residents' faces light-up when they see the children participate. The service seating is arranged in a circle for maximum face-to-face interaction. Even some of the most cognitively impaired residents hum along to the familiar hymns.

The Ministry of Praise, sponsored by St. Camillus Catholic Church, is a prayer group begun by the Archdiocese of Chicago to create a sense of belonging to a faith community for those unable to fully participate in church services due to medical and mental incapacities. Those wishing to belong are commissioned as Ministers of Praise at a special Mass at the nursing home. They are given prayer books, a cross from the Holy Land, and a certificate of membership. They also receive a monthly newsletter encouraging prayers for specific intentions.

A number of our residents use their prayer books each day and wear their crosses as a symbol of their belonging. The residents often express that they are thankful to be able to participate in the Church's work although confined to the home. St. Camillus also has a Mass on the third Thursday of the month, and sends flowers for the residents at Easter and Christmas.

The Beltsville Seventh-Day Adventist School has an intergenerational program that sends their students into the community once a month for religious musical performances. The children sing songs, play piano, and distribute cards that they have made for the residents. The residents respond with smiles, singing aloud to the music and applause in appreciation. Mrs. Wolford, the students' teacher, has been bringing her students to the Althea Woodland for over five years. The residents look forward to the lively young students who share their enthusiasm for God.

The Jewish Chaplaincy Service of the Greater Washington Area supports our Jewish residents with holiday cards, prayer books and volunteers for services and programs about the Jewish faith. For example, during this Passover season, four young girls from the Yeshiva visited our residents to organize a simple Seder and explain the holiday through prayers and song. All the residents of the home were invited and many non-Jewish residents attended. They listened intently to the readings and enjoyed sampling the traditional foods of the Seder. The Jewish residents nodded their heads in agreement and talked about their own Seders in the past. It gave them a sense of reconnecting to their past when they reminisced about their lives.

Two different Bible studies are held at the Althea Woodland. One, led by Joyce Coffin from the Church of the Atonement, is held each Monday morning. Each week a different Bible theme is explored using readings, prayers, and the sharing of experiences that are then reinforced with prayer cards, songs, and praying with each resident. Her approach uses all the senses to draw out and involve even the most withdrawn resident to feel the love and peace of God in their life.

Reverend DeKalb, from Clifton Park Baptist Church, shares Bible readings twice a month that begin with the story of creation and continue through the Old Testament. Residents express the feelings of comfort they receive listening to the familiar stories.

Chris Romig, sophomore at Princeton Theological Seminary, has been volunteering at the Althea Woodland since he was in junior high school. He ministers to our residents with his individual visits, musical performances, and birthday remembrances. His empathetic, gentle, and understanding nature are a blessing to our residents, families, and staff. He has been presider at a Memorial Service for our deceased residents that celebrated their lives with prayers, music, and a "Bouquet of Love" which gave an opportunity for the staff, residents, and families to share memories about the deceased. Ideas for the format of the service were taken from *Dealing Creatively With Death* (Morgan, 1984).

CHALLENGES

Many problems can arise when so many different faiths and people are involved in religious programs. Careful volunteer orientation is necessary to maintain order and maximum benefit for residents.

All residents are invited to attend any religious group, therefore sensitivity to special needs and appropriate behaviors during the individual services are monitored by staff and volunteers so as not to offend or disturb other residents. For example, residents who may have difficulty listening quietly during a service may need someone to sit with them or walk them out if need be.

Volunteers can be made aware of any special physical needs, such as breaking the communion wafer into smaller pieces to aid receiving. Adult volunteers are cautioned about bringing in children who may be actively exhibiting cold or flu symptoms. This is to remind them of our residents' lower resistance to disease.

CONCLUSION

Religious volunteers provide an invaluable service to residents of nursing homes who otherwise may feel forgotten, alienated or in spiritual distress. "When all else goes, spirituality remains. It's a strength that can remain with us to the end" says Eugene C. Bianchi, religion professor at Emory University (*Washington Post*, 1995).

Each resident, no matter how physically or mentally impaired, can benefit from appropriate religious programming. The later years of life and the dying process itself can be one of "spiritual completion" through "spiritual eldering" says Rabbi Zalman Schacter-Shalomi in an interview in the *Washington Post* (Rifin, 1995). He calls it "turning the elderly into elders." An appropriate religious volunteer program will enhance the quality of life for nursing home residents by the fostering of empowerment, maintaining a sense of spiritual and mental well-being, and providing solace to those in need.

AUTHOR NOTE

Janet Grenon Ragno, ADC, received her Bachelor of Psychology degree from the University of Maryland in 1988. Ms. Ragno is a Level II certified catechist through the Archdiocese of Washington, D.C. and has taught Special Religious Education at St. Patrick's Parish in Norbeck, Maryland. She has also held positions as Religious Education Coordinator in a military interdenominational chapel in Stuttgart, West Germany and Youth Coordinator at Walnut Hill Baptist Church in Petersburg, Virginia. She resides in Silver Spring, Maryland with her daughter Janelle.

REFERENCES

The Federal Register. (1991). The Interpretive Guidelines, *56*(187) Washington, D.C.: AHCA.

Kalina, K. (1993). *Midwife for Souls: Spiritual Care for the Dying.* Boston, MA: St. Paul Books and Media.

Ministry of Praise. (Undated). Chicago, Ill: National Office of the Ministry of Praise.

Morgan, E. (1984). *Dealing Creatively with Death: A Manual of Death Education and Simple Burial.* Burnsville, NC: Celo Press.

Rifin, L. (1995, March 25). A satisfying conclusion. *The Washington Post.* p. B7.

Adopt An Elder:
Linking Youth and the Elderly

Gwen Waggoner

SUMMARY. Adopt An Elder is a volunteer intergenerational program designed to dispel misconceptions of aging, and to provide for selected teens an understanding of the normal aging process, as well as the diminished physical and mental abilities of individuals with Alzheimer's disease and other forms of dementia. Personal experiences of former teen volunteers are cited. Discussion presents methods to sensitively address the needs of both teens and the elderly. *[Article copies available from The Haworth Document Delivery Service: 1-800-342-9678.]*

America is a nation that is rapidly aging. Individuals over 85 are the fastest growing segment of our population; in the next 60 years their

Gwen Waggoner is Director of Special Projects for The French Foundation for Alzheimer Research in Los Angeles, CA.

Address correspondence to the author at: 3263 Colony Circle, Los Angeles, CA 90027.

[Haworth co-indexing entry note]: "Adopt An Elder: Linking Youth and the Elderly," Waggoner, Gwen. Co-published simultaneously in *Activities, Adaptation & Aging* (The Haworth Press, Inc.) Vol. 20, No. 1, 1995, pp. 41-52; and: *Volunteerism in Geriatric Settings* (ed: Vera R. Jackson), The Haworth Press, Inc., 1995, pp. 41-52. Single or multiple copies of this article/chapter may be purchased from The Haworth Document Delivery Center [1-800-342-9678, 9:00 a.m. - 5:00 p.m. (EST)].

41

numbers will increase almost fivefold to 16.1 million, or about 5 percent of the population (Gilford, 1988). Hand in hand with our rapidly growing aging population are myriad health care challenges. One of these is dementia. It has been suggested by Cross and Gurland (1986) that severe dementia affects as many as 25 percent of those 85 or older. Projections based on a recent study of the Congressional Advisory Panel on Alzheimer's Disease suggest that by the year 2040 the number of cases of Alzheimer's disease (the most prevalent of the dementias) may exceed 6 million.

There is already a severe shortage of health care professionals overall, especially in the field of care of the elderly. Based on the above projections, the need for qualified professionals to care for the elderly in general, and specifically those afflicted with a form of dementia, will be dramatically magnified over the next several years. This paper offers one approach that The French Foundation for Alzheimer Research in Los Angeles, California has developed to address this need.

OVERVIEW

Adopt An Elder is a volunteer community service program which has had a successful history since the summer of 1991. Geographical location for the program is determined through a variety of avenues: A particular facility learns about the program and wants to be a participant . . . a local high school or youth organization sees the program as a positive and worthy experience for their teens . . . an individual, corporation or civic group is desirous of supporting an outreach program involving the youth of their community and views Adopt An Elder as an effective vehicle for accomplishing that.

Through an application and personal interview process, high school juniors and seniors are recruited and assigned to volunteer a designated number of hours as "junior interns" in pre-determined local facilities. These facilities span the range of senior independent living, adult day care, skilled nursing, and Alzheimer's care. A local university student is recruited to serve as coordinator/mentor of the program.

Following the selection process, prior to beginning work assignments in the facilities, junior interns attend a mandatory two days of training. Once on site, facilities' staff closely supervise junior interns as they perform a wide range of duties. The main objective for teens involved in this volunteer project is to be a caring, empathetic friend to the elderly whom they encounter. This objective is met through many forms . . . simply sitting with a client or resident, providing companionship; reading to those with failing eyesight; providing physical support to weakened legs in the process of relocating from one place to another; assisting a wheelchair-bound client or resident outside for a little fresh air and sunshine; motivating isolated elderly to join activities; helping write and/or read letters; or listening as one reminisces about the past. As a result, the generation gap is bridged and a unique bond is formed.

The program time frame varies with each implementation. Most frequently it falls within a normal school semester, with students working after school and on weekends. In other instances it runs as a summer program when students have the flexibility of working more weekday hours. A small scholarship incentive is built into the program to spur interest in participation.

An ongoing journal of work experience is required of all junior interns throughout their involvement in the program, and at the program's conclusion evaluation forms are distributed to all involved parties.

MISSION

The mission of the Adopt An Elder program is to provide for young people:

- Exposure to healthy elderly and to the rewarding experience of interaction with them.
- Education regarding physical and mental decline which is part of the normal aging process.
- Encouragement to develop a sense of understanding and patience with characteristics of the aging process.
- Understanding of the unique aspects of physical and mental decline associated with those suffering from various forms of dementia–with special emphasis on Alzheimer's disease.
- Hands-on experience which will inspire interest to pursue a career in care of the elderly–specifically those afflicted with Alzheimer's disease.

FACILITIES (WORK SITES)

The selection of facilities to serve as work sites for junior intern volunteer participants in the Adopt An Elder program is made after careful consideration of several possibilities. Ideally, you want a clean, cheerful facility where clients/residents are treated with respect and dignity, with a caring staff who love and take pride in what they do. It is important that these young volunteers see the reality of many of the nation's facilities for care of the elderly where they are operating with limited funds and insufficient and overworked staff. At the same time, this is to be a positive experience for them so a delicate balance is the goal in selection of each work site.

Adopt An Elder is designed to expose the young volunteers to the normal progression of decline in the aging process. Senior Residential Living complexes provide interaction with healthy elderly in settings where they live very independently. Adult Day Care centers take them to the next level, exposing them to those who have increased limitations and special physical, mental and emotional needs. A Skilled Nursing Facility, where 24-hour care is provided, takes them to yet another dimension of their experience. The fourth component is the Alzheimer's unit or facility setting. It is in this environment that they become acutely aware of the unique needs of those afflicted with Alzheimer's disease and other forms of dementia. It is not always necessary to have four separate facilities participating in the program. Frequently more than one of the four necessary components can be found within one facility, i.e., skilled nursing and Alzheimer's unit.

In each setting the junior interns work with full-time and part-time staff, as well as adult volunteers. This exposure allows them to observe and experience the rewards of a career in the field of care of the elderly, as well as the personal satisfaction and "good feeling" of long-term volunteering.

The initial approach to facilities to solicit participation in the Adopt An Elder program is frequently met with some resistance. Nearly all have had a negative experience with volunteers–especially teen volunteers. Well-meaning church groups, youth organizations, etc., have decided they want their youth to have experience in volunteering among the elderly and have sent them to the facility with no screening to determine interest and capabilities, no training and preparation, no structure of scheduling, and leaving the full load of supervision and monitoring on the already over-whelmed facilities staff. It is the strict criteria and guidelines for junior interns, the application and personal interview process, and the detailed mandatory training that assures facilities that great emphasis is placed on preparation for volunteer service in the Adopt An Elder program. The fact that a specific individual coordinates schedules, monitors performance and is available to facilities staff for problem-solving, if necessary, lends further strength to the Adopt An Elder program.

Not all facilities who commit to involvement in this program fulfill their commitment as agreed. In some instances the staff is non-directive, resulting in confusion on the part of the young volunteers. In other instances some staff may resent the presence of the junior interns and treat them unkindly. There have been cases where the teen volunteers have observed less than appropriate treatment of residents by staff or lack of attention to a patient who is "wet" and, in reporting the situation, have been told "That is none of your business." As specific issues of breakdown become known they are addressed on an individual basis. Overall, however, facilities have been very cooperative and conscientious in their commitment to the success of the program.

There are many benefits to facilities who become work sites for Adopt An Elder junior interns. These include freshness and vitality of youth, additional hands to help facilitate efforts, one-on-one attention for socially isolated clients and residents, and enhanced activities.

RECRUITMENT

When the geographical area of the project has been determined and participating facilities selected, the next step is to locate a high school within close proximity of the facilities. (A local youth organization or church youth group are other options.) Officials of that school are then approached as a possible avenue for student recruitment. Many high schools have a Community Service Program or Community Based Learning Program built into their curriculum and choose to include Adopt An Elder as part of that existing process. Others offer the program to their students strictly as an extracurricular volunteer opportunity. Once commitment to the program is received application packages are prepared for distribution.

The application package includes a description of the program; location of participating facilities; mission statement; criteria for prospective junior interns (at least 16 years of age . . . minimum grade point average of 2.5 . . . reliable school attendance and punctuality record); request for a one page statement of interest in the program; two confidential letters of recommendation from former or current teachers, counselors, youth organization leaders, clergy or employers; parent/guardian approval; and personal interview.

Size of the program (number of participants accepted) varies according to funds available for that particular project. Number of junior interns in a given program, to date, has been as few as 4 and as many as 16.

What is it about the Adopt An Elder program that appeals to teens and makes them want to become involved? One writes in her statement of interest in the program, "I wish to become a participant in this program because I want to help the elderly in any way I can, and to make them feel happy, loved and wanted. I think it is very sad that some families won't take care of their elders. They need attention and love just like the rest of the family. I think I can learn a lot from the elderly people. I know that I will have the satisfaction of knowing that I helped the elderly feel special." Another said, "I am very excited about becoming a part of the Adopt An Elder program. I don't only feel that this will benefit the people and elders involved, but I see how I could benefit immensely from them and their experiences." Yet another stated "I want to be a part of the elder people's lives. By sharing my experiences with them and listening to their life stories, I hope to create a bond between our generations. By taking part in this program, I hope to develop the patience, appreciation and understanding the elderly need."

It is important to state here that the very design of the application package is such that it would have appeal only to responsible teens desirous of reaching out to others in the community. The program description, personal criteria which must be met, and guidelines for participation discourages consideration of the self-involved and those who lack the personal discipline to be faithful to a commitment.

JOURNAL

A journal of work experience is required of each junior intern. It is suggested that each day they return from a work assignment they jot down a few sentences regarding their feelings and attitudes about their interaction with clients/residents and staff that particular day. This regular documentation of their experiences contributes to the personal growth of the junior intern, and it serves as a gauge to monitor the success of the program.

SCHOLARSHIP

Upon completion of a specified number of hours within an individual program a nominal scholarship is placed in reserve at The French Foundation for Alzheimer Research. Number of hours required and amount of scholarship varies. On average, for a total of 100-120 volunteer hours, a $300 scholarship has been provided. This scholarship is released to the junior intern upon receipt of documentation of college entrance (letter of acceptance, receipt of tuition or book dues paid, etc.). Community College, Junior College and Vocational School are acceptable.

The scholarship amount is a factor in determining funding needed for the project. The $300 amount is, admittedly, not large, but keep in mind that this is a *volunteer* project. The policy of holding the scholarship funds until documentation of college entrance is received is to encourage further education.

When one junior intern volunteer was asked in the evaluation process "How important to you were the award incentives?" she responded "Somewhat important in the beginning. Now it doesn't matter at all." This is what we hope for. The scholarship may be the incentive needed to get someone involved in the program. Once they become involved, the personal satisfaction and joy they receive renders any monetary reward unimportant.

COORDINATOR/MENTOR

The role of coordinator/mentor is usually filled by a Social Work practicum student recruited from a local university. (A nursing student with a goal to enter the field of gerontology is another option.) It is important to find one who is planning for a career in gerontology, has a vital interest in both teens and the elderly, and shows evidence of being able to work well with both. Availability and willingness to spend evening and weekend hours mentoring the junior intern volunteers is also critical in this selection process.

In this role, the practicum student coordinates junior interns' schedules with the participating facilities, meets weekly with the junior interns, monitors their performance at the facilities and serves as mentor to them throughout the project.

The role of mentoring the junior interns is a most important one. The Adopt an Elder program offers an experience which will be new and foreign to some, and one which will be approached with a considerable degree of apprehension and fear. Others may come from homes where there is little discipline and accountability. Some will be shy and insecure. Others will be strong-willed and have a tendency to want to perform within the program according to their own rules. Whatever the situation, each junior intern volunteer will need patient counsel, guidance, and encouragement along the way. For the duration of the program the coordinator/mentor makes *frequent* contact with each junior intern (ideally once a week or every two weeks.) In addition, it is important that the entire group meet together periodically for a sort of "group therapy" session. The coordinator/mentor initiates and facilitates interaction, allowing junior interns to talk about their experiences in a setting where they feel safe and comfortable, knowing they are not alone in their feelings and attitudes.

The practicum student benefits from hands-on experience with the teen volunteers, as well as staff and volunteers within the facilities. The practicum student also receives credit toward his/her degree for hours worked on the Adopt An Elder project.

TRAINING/CELEBRATION EVENT

Training material for the Adopt An Elder program was designed by and is presented by Ellen Knuff, registered nurse and educator in the field of gerontology, with special emphasis on dementia. Ms. Knuff's nursing career, which spans three decades, includes work in long-term care, respite care and office nursing. The intense two days of training, which precedes the first day of junior interns' work in the facilities, covers "Normal Aging," "Abnormal Aging: The Dementias," and Communicating with A Dementia Resident." Having personally toured the participating facilities prior to training, Ms. Knuff is able to personalize the training to prepare junior interns as much as possible for specific conditions and situations they will find in their work assignments. Junior interns are actively involved throughout the training, with considerable time spent in role-playing.

At the conclusion of training a celebration event is held to honor the junior interns. Among those attending this event are junior interns, parents, coordinator/mentor, representatives from participating facilities, training instructor, and representatives from the sponsoring organization. A certificate of completion of training is presented to each junior intern. Facilities' representatives have an opportunity to meet the junior interns and personally welcome them to join their staff and volunteers in meeting the individual needs of their clients and residents. This is a celebratory event of junior intern recognition, affirmation, congratulations, and encouragement as they set out to begin their volunteer assignments.

VOLUNTEER BENEFITS

Even though the junior interns, through pre-service training, have been prepared for the situations they will find in their actual work assignments and taught how to deal with those situations, they enter the facilities for the first time with a great deal of apprehension. Very quickly, however, they are very much at ease with both staff and clients/residents and performing their duties with great confidence and poise.

Through interaction with the clients and residents, and working with various staff members and adult volunteers at the facilities, each junior intern volunteer benefits greatly from this experience in areas such as:

- accountability
- confidentiality
- understanding of the aging process
- patience
- sensitivity
- concern and care for others
- the right of the elderly to be treated with respect and dignity
- increased self-esteem

Throughout the weeks and months of a particular program solid relationships are formed between teen volunteers and the elderly whom they visit regularly after school and on weekends. Friendships develop and attitudes change. Kelly G. reflects on her experience in the Adopt An Elder program. "It's just like being a friend to anybody else, really. You see someone who was okay one week and now they're in a bed the next, or you go back in and someone doesn't remember you. You can have really hard days, but I feel so good about doing this."

"When you go in there, their eyes light up," states junior intern Jude C. "They just love to see people."

Shanna P. says, "After working at the two facilities I find myself being more aware of and attentive to elderly people in every circumstance–grocery store, park, on the street–I don't look at them the same as I used to. I kind of smile to myself and often wonder 'What's their story?' or 'Where are they going?' I think I see them as *real* people."

At the conclusion of the program in Anchorage, Alaska, high school senior Kelly H. evaluated her experience of junior internship. When asked "What did you enjoy most?" Kelly responded "Seeing people improve physically and mentally due to my encouragement. Having people light up when I would come in." When asked to comment on the importance of the project to her personally Kelly said, "I love my new friends. I'm so glad I became involved so I now know how to deal with all kinds of people and love all kinds of people." It is truly a delight to see the transformation in these young people, and the joy they bring to the elderly.

One of the long-term benefits of the program is that, through hands-on experience in the facilities, these young volunteers will be made aware of health care for the elderly as a viable and rewarding career option, most worthy of their consideration.

EVALUATION

At the conclusion of each Adopt An Elder program evaluation forms are distributed to junior interns, parents/guardians, participating facilities' staff, coordinator/mentor, and participating school officials. The evaluator responds to questions regarding the congruence of program mission, goals, and achievements in both process and outcome. The evaluation also includes strengths, weaknesses, and benefits as observed and experienced by each participating entity.

Periodically, a local university is approached to identify a professional investigator to conduct an independent evaluation of this program.

RETENTION

To date, retention rate in the Adopt An Elder program has been outstanding. In all but two programs, 100% of teen volunteers in the program went on to complete the required hours. One of the other two resulted in 83% retention. The other, the initial pilot program involving many inner city youth, ended with 57% retention. The main reason for failure to complete the program has been a situation of overwhelming family responsibilities. These young people were in a single parent situation where the parent had to work and the teen had responsibilities caring for younger siblings. Others find themselves overcommitted with the combination of school, part-time jobs, family and their volunteer commitments. They have simply taken on more than they can handle–physically, mentally and emotionally. The degree of parent/guardian support is a significant factor in retention rate. It is with this in mind that parents/guardians are invited to the celebration event following training so that they might better understand the program and be supportive of their teen participant.

It is believed that the retention success of this program, thus far, can be attributed to clear definition of the program as it is presented to potential teen participants, the personal interview where specific concerns can be addressed, an effective training process, careful selection of participating facilities, and faithful guidance of the coordinator/mentor.

FUNDING

As with all projects, there are expenses involved in implementing the Adopt An Elder program. Community service is important to any locale, and an intergenerational project has growing appeal to the community now being forced to acknowledge our aging population, and the resulting needs. Adopt An Elder has received warm response from major corporations who are willing to provide the necessary finances to bring the program to their cities and communities. Other options for funding are civic groups and individuals. The key is to make potential sources of funding aware of the existence of the program, and the successful record of implementation. Quotations of previous junior intern volunteers are most effective in showing that this program results in a positive impact on participants and the local community, and that it is one most worthy of their financial support.

CONCLUSION

A recent study conducted by Independent Sector in Washington, D.C. concluded that children who volunteer become adults who volunteer, passing values on to the next generation.

At a time when the media seems obsessed with the negative attitudes and actions of youth in our society it is heartwarming, indeed, to see the sensitivity and sincere desire of many teens to reach out to their community and give of themselves in a loving and caring manner. The attention Adopt An Elder teens give the elderly whom they encounter in their volunteer work assignments results in increased joy and self-esteem for those who frequently receive little one-on-one attention. The lasting impact on the young people themselves is immeasurable.

The Adopt An Elder program is a major effort on the part of The French Foundation for Alzheimer Research to address the staggering impact of our rapidly growing aging population, and the concurrent increasing number of Alzheimer's victims. We must do all we can to challenge the youth of today to consider care of the elderly as a viable career option. For those who participate in the program and ultimately decide on another career direction, we have the assurance that, as a result of their Adopt An Elder volunteer experience, they will have greater understanding of the aging process and the devastating impact of Alzheimer's disease, and have much more empathy for the elderly and the wide scope of their needs.

AUTHOR NOTE

Gwen Waggoner is a graduate of Moody Bible Institute in Chicago with emphasis on education and music, and has taken undergraduate studies in communications and psychology at UCLA. Ms. Waggoner hosted a daily radio talk show for 8 years, and has 4 years experience in television production. She has been employed by several non-profit organizations where her responsibilities included the supervision of volunteers. Among her own volunteer experience is California Special Olympics and Centrum of Hollywood, an organization for teenage runaways. Ms. Waggoner developed Adopt an Elder and directs implementation of each program. (Adopt An Elder concept and funding procurement by Thomas M. Ennis, President of The French Foundation for Alzheimer Research.)

REFERENCES

Advisory Panel on Alzheimer's Disease. *Report of the Advisory Panel on Alzheimer's Disease*, 1988-1989. DHHS Pub. No. (ADM) 89-1644. Washington, DC: Supt. of Docs., U.S. Govt. Print. Off., 1989.

Cross, P.S., and Gurland, B.J. "The Epidemiology of Dementing Disorders." Contract report prepared for the Office of Technology Assessment, U.S. Congress, 1986.

Gilford, D.M. ed. *(The Aging Population in the Twenty-First Century: Statistics for Health Policy.* Washington, DC: National Academy Press, 1988).

Culinary Delights from Around the World
(International Cuisine Volunteer Program)

Darlene J. Bruton

SUMMARY. This program involves teaching simple cooking techniques to senior citizens within nursing care facilities. The participants
in the program would explore the foods of various countries. Lessons
would be taught by volunteers, from local communities and from area
high schools which surround the nursing care facility being served. In
some instances special guests would be invited to demonstrate foods
from a particular country. Volunteers would require the guidance and
support of the nursing care facility's management staff. *[Article copies
available from The Haworth Document Delivery Service: 1-800-342-9678.]*

It is good food and not fine words that keep me alive.

– Moliere

INTRODUCTION

Everyone needs food to survive. Hence, the enjoyment of food is a
common link among all people regardless of place or circumstance.

Darlene J. Bruton is President of the Bruton Group and a teacher candidate in
the Teacher Cerification Program in Business Education at the University of
Maryland.
Address correspondence to the author at: P.O. Box 243, Hyattsville, MD
20781-0243.

[Haworth co-indexing entry note]: "Culinary Delights from Around the World (International Cuisine Volunteer Program)," Bruton, Darlene J. Co-published simultaneously in *Activities, Adaptation &
Aging* (The Haworth Press, Inc.) Vol. 20, No. 1, 1995, pp. 53-69; and: *Volunteerism in Geriatric Settings*
(ed: Vera R. Jackson), The Haworth Press, Inc., 1995, pp. 53-69. Single or multiple copies of this
article/chapter may be purchased from The Haworth Document Delivery Center [1-800-342-9678, 9:00
a.m. - 5:00 p.m. (EST)].

53

The Culinary Delights from Around the World program is designed to challenge, stimulate and revitalize senior citizens who reside in nursing care facilities. The program would enable residents to participate in an international cuisine volunteer program which would focus on the people, the land and the food of various countries. The program would be entertaining, but more importantly, it would provide an air of familiarity for some of the residents who may miss spending time in the kitchen.

The array of countries to be studied would be unlimited. Selection of countries may be systematic, arbitrary or may be recommended by program participants.

The Culinary Delights from Around the World program is an eight-week "hands on" program that will meet one day a week. A new program may commence every eight weeks or another section may run concurrently. The program is divided into eight, one and one-half hour sessions. Each session would consist of a fifteen minute overview of the country–the geographical region, the people and their customs and the food they cook and eat. To enhance the presentation, the volunteer team will make every effort to simulate the country, including wearing a costume descriptive of the country being studied. The remaining one hour and fifteen minutes would be used to prepare and eat sample dishes. Residents may be unable to complete a full menu because of the time constraints, but the volunteer team should seek diversity when planning dishes and/or menus. The residents may prepare desserts, appetizers, light snacks or light meals. Some preparations may be made ahead of time.

The ideal group size for this program would be eight to ten residents. Although group size may vary, it should remain small enough to create an intimacy among the program participants. To participate in the program, residents should be mobile and should be on a regular diet. The volunteer coordinator will consult with the dietary staff to ensure that menu selections do not conflict with a resident's dietary program.

To ensure the smooth operation of the program, each volunteer student will select a resident as a buddy and will work with that person exclusively during the cooking sessions. The success of the Culinary Delights from Around the World program rests on the volunteer team's ability to involve the residents and to get them to share and to interact with their fellow residents.

THE VOLUNTEER TEAM

Volunteer Coordinator. The volunteer coordinator will spearhead the Culinary Delights from Around the World program. This person should have direct responsibility for planning and implementing the program, developing fundraising strategies and marketing techniques, recruiting student volunteers and consulting routinely with the appropriate nursing care facility staff. The volunteer coordinator will work closely with the facility's activity director to keep him or her informed of the program.

The volunteer coordinator need not be a professional chef or nutritionist, but (s)he should have an interest in cooking and some general knowledge about nutrition. This person should have a strong interest in working with people, have good human relations, planning and organizational skills and be adept at working with diverse groups.

The activity director of the nursing care facility would recruit the volunteer coordinator from the community or from a local university. This would provide an excellent opportunity for a homemaker or a retired person. It would also provide an excellent opportunity for someone in an undergraduate or graduate program who is seeking field placement experience. A student in any of the following majors might enjoy overseeing this program: home economics, business administration, social work, nutrition/dietary sciences and health care administration; however, selection would not be limited to these majors. The volunteer coordinator should be prepared to spend five to ten hours per week on this program. There may be times during the initial implementation phase when additional hours would be required.

Student Volunteers. The volunteer coordinator would be enlisted to contact local high schools to elicit the help of students interested in performing community service. This person would work with an appointed staff person at the school to select and to schedule students. Although there are no formal requirements for being selected to participate in the program, a student should have an interest in working with the elderly, have a good attitude and be adaptable. In addition, a student should be committed to working up to two hours per week for a full session of the Culinary Delights from Around the World program which is eight weeks. The volunteer coordinator and the student volunteers would comprise the volunteer team and would be responsible for planning and implementing each session.

PROGRAM ENVIRONMENT

The program will be held in the facility's dining area adjacent to the kitchen. If at all possible, a small private room in close proximity to the kitchen would be preferable. The volunteer coordinator should consult with the activity director and other appropriate staff to determine the location, day and time of the weekly session. The session should be scheduled at a time that does not interfere with overall meal preparations for facility residents. Also, the volunteer coordinator should work with the kitchen staff to determine what cooking utensils may be utilized by the program.

PROGRAM RESOURCES

The Culinary Delights from Around the World program would be a self-sufficient program within the nursing care facility. The program would not receive funds from the general operating budget of the facility, unless the facility earmarks funds for such recreational programs.

The volunteer coordinator would be responsible for developing fundraising activities to raise money for food and supplies to run the program. Fundraising efforts might involve the solicitation of funds from local area businesses. This effort would include a well-planned, written and oral campaign. The volunteer coordinator would also try to establish a relationship with local area supermarkets and specialty food stores in order to obtain gift certificates and/or discounts on food items and supplies. Another fundraising idea would be to contact local area restaurants to ask that they sponsor an international meal for the program participants. In this instance, the restaurant would send someone to conduct a demonstration and to aid residents in the preparation of an ethnic meal. The food and any supplies needed would be donated by the restaurant. A similar approach could be used with pastry shops and/or bakeries.

A long-term fundraising effort would be the compilation of favorite recipes which would be submitted by a facility's residents. This would not have to be limited to program participants. Program participants could ask their friends to submit their favorite recipes as well. Each recipe could be personalized by adding a short piece about its significance to the person who submitted it. After the cookbook is put together, orders would be taken to sell it. The volunteers and the nursing care facility's staff would work to market the cookbook to the community. All proceeds would be retained for the program.

The volunteer coordinator would seek the assistance of the facility's chief financial officer to set up financial records and a checking account for the program. The chief financial officer would provide a financial statement to the activity director and the volunteer coordinator on a monthly basis.

MENUS WITH NUTRITIONAL VALUE

In a nursing care facility a primary consideration is the health of the residents. Menu selection must provide for a nutritionally balanced diet and for special needs such as low-fat, low-sodium or calorie-controlled diets. It must also take into consideration different cultural and ethnic backgrounds which result in certain food likes and dislikes and religious restrictions.

The volunteer team, in consultation with the dietary staff of the nursing care facility, will select the menu prior to each session. Menus will meet the psychological, social, nutritional and aesthetic needs of the residents.

Menus may be basic and simple or exciting and time-consuming. The detail and complexity of menus will be based on the time format selected (suggested timeframes would be one and one-half hour or two-hours) for each session. If the shorter time format is selected, a sampler, single dish or light meal might be prepared. A two-hour time format would enable greater menu selection and flexibility, but may be a little tiring for the residents. The volunteer team may handle some food preparations prior to the session in order for residents to complete the meal and to eat it within the allowable timeframe. Menu suggestions for the next session may be taken from the residents. All efforts should be taken to include any suggestions received.

PURCHASING AND STORING FOOD

The volunteer coordinator will be responsible for purchasing all food items for the program. Quality food products will be purchased from local grocery stores in the area. All food items will be purchased with an eye toward quality, safety and sanitation of food.

In most instances, food for the cooking program will be purchased and brought into the nursing care facility the day of the session. Therefore, appropriate short-term food storage would be required. The volunteer coordinator will work with the kitchen staff to ensure that all food items have the right light, temperature, ventilation, air movement and refrigeration. The volunteer coordinator will work with nursing care staff to ensure that any government regulations related to food handling and preparation are followed.

SAMPLE OF LESSON PLAN STRUCTURE

The lesson plan can be simple or detailed. The idea is to share information about the country being studied in an interesting way. The lesson plan, however, should include everything that will be done for the session so that it is conducted in an organized manner. Failure to be thorough in planning might lead to a disastrous session. Use the lesson plan as a road map beginning at one point and ending at another. Below are some ideas about what could be included in the lesson plan. Lesson content may be changed to make the study more interesting.

- Lesson: International Cuisine–(Name the country)
- Meal to be prepared: List menu selections and the number of people to be served.
- Ingredients needed: All ingredients and amounts should be listed.
- Cooking utensils and supplies: All necessary items should be listed.
- Items needed for table service: List items needed such as tablecloth, silverware, plates, saucers, glasses, centerpiece and so on.
- Laboratory assignments: Assign residents specific responsibilities for assisting in the preparation of the meal. Each resident will be paired with his/her buddy.
- General objective: Residents will gain a better understanding of how the land, the people and the customs impact upon the types of foods cooked in a particular country.
- Supporting objectives: (1) Residents will be able to identify the food customs of a particular country and describe the reasons for the customs; (2) Residents will be able to demonstrate the ability to prepare and serve international foods; (3) Residents will be able to identify ways of being creative when preparing international foods; and (4) Residents will be able to share their own personal experiences as they relate to ethnic background, culture and foods.
- Lesson format: Describe the method to be used to teach the lesson. Any one or combination of the following may be used: lecture, demonstration, skit, video, personal reflections of the residents, special guests and other visual aids.
- Lesson content: This is only a guide of what might be included in a lesson.

    I. Overview of the Country

        A. History
        B. Geographical influences
          1. Location of country
          2. Climate
        C. Impact of the land on agricultural products
        D. Diversity of the people
        E. Cultural influences

II. The food–What the people eat and why

   A. Typical foods
   B. Special cooking methods
   C. Religious restrictions
   D. Special festivals and foods

III. Meal and Meal Service

- Learning activities: This would include activities the residents would be involved in as a part of the program. Some examples of learning activities would be as follows:

  1. Select a country, research the geography, the people, the culture and the food. Relate findings to food customs.
  2. Develop a scrapbook of favorite recipes from each country. Include a brief write up highlighting the customs and the rituals. This could be expanded for a fundraising activity.
  3. Provide laboratory experience to residents to prepare dishes and foods of various countries.

- Meal preparation and service: The volunteer coordinator will distribute the menus and assignments to each pair (resident and student). All instructions for the meal preparation should be organized and clear. The volunteer coordinator will circulate among the groups to make sure the meal is being prepared as planned and will lend assistance whenever needed. After all dishes have been prepared and the tables set, everyone will have an opportunity to eat what has been prepared.
- Clean up: Each group should be assigned clean up responsibilities.
- Lesson wrap up: The volunteer coordinator will briefly recap the day's session. It is important to assess what the residents felt about the session. Take under advisement any suggestions offered. The volunteer coordinator will also preview the next lesson and entertain suggestions and contributions from the residents.

PROGRAM MATERIALS

Reference books and recipes will be the primary materials needed for teaching the lessons and preparing the menus. The local public library has a large selection of books and other references on international cuisine. Almost any of these books would have recipes that could be used in the program, but the key is to find recipes that are simple and easy to make.

One of the best series of cookbooks may be found in the children's section at the public library. There are twenty-six *Easy Menu Ethnic Cookbooks* in the series. Each features a different country and provides information on the country, including the history, the people, the customs, the food, special holidays, festivals and religious observances. There is also information on cooking utensils, cooking terms, special ingredients, recipes and complete menus. Examples of books in the series are: *Cooking the African Way, Cooking the Australian Way, Cooking the Austrian Way, Desserts Around the World and Holiday Cooking Around the World.*

Another good cookbook is Sheila Lukins' *All Around the World Cookbook.* This cookbook is over 500 pages of fun and excitement. In addition to great recipes, Sheila Lukins shares her personal experiences of travels around the world and her passion for global cuisine.

If further information is needed on the country to be studied, almost any reference book would have the information necessary for the program.

SAMPLE RECIPES

Recipes that appear in the *Easy Menu Ethnic Cookbooks* are listed in Appendix A to this program narrative. Recipes were chosen randomly and represent the following countries: Africa, Korea, Italy, South America, Russia and France. These recipes are simple and easy to make. If the instructions are followed, they are quite reliable and could be used to start the program. Since these are single dishes, other foods may be added to make a full menu, i.e., bread, salad, beverage. Additionally, preparation may be needed for some recipes prior to the session in order that there is enough time to complete preparation of the dish and to eat.

BENEFITS TO THE NURSING CARE FACILITY

The Culinary Delights from Around the World program would require very little physical work or time on the part of a nursing care facility staff which might already feel stretched by current responsibilities. The primary role of the staff, in particular, the activity director, would be to facilitate the program. Specifically, the activity director would serve as liaison between the volunteer coordinator and the other staff (dietary, kitchen, recreation). The volunteer coordinator would work closely with the activity director to ensure that the program does not violate any facility guidelines, policies or procedures. The Culinary Delights from Around the World program would be planned and implemented by the volunteer team.

This program will show the public at large as well as prospective residents and their families the extent to which the facility will attempt to provide stimulating recreational activities and programs for its residents. Further, it will show that the facility has an interest in providing more than just routine care and maintenance.

From a public relations standpoint, implementation of this program would create a link with the community by providing activities that foster community support and assistance. People on the outside actually get to look in at the good and positive activities that the facility offers. Limited resources continue to be a constant and nagging problem for many nursing care facilities and similar organizations. Having a volunteer program of this magnitude would enable the facility to offer a program which would not burden or put stress on the current financial position of the facility.

BENEFITS TO STUDENT VOLUNTEERS

Most high school students have had very little interaction with senior citizens other than perhaps with grandparents or aunts and uncles. Consequently, many students view senior citizens as a mystery.

The Culinary Delights from Around the World program will provide an excellent opportunity for local area high school students to gain insight into the lives of senior citizens and to receive firsthand experience interacting with them and assisting them. By giving their time, the students will help to make the residents' lives a little brighter. The buddy system will provide an even greater opportunity for each student to bond with a resident of the facility. It is no secret that everyone likes to have someone make them feel special. This applies twofold with senior citizens who often have few or infrequent visitors. Students will be able to make a positive contribution to the community and, at the same time, satisfy their community service requirements if the school district requires it.

BENEFITS TO RESIDENTS

Residents have passed the point in their lives where daily meal planning and preparation are at the top of their list of things to do. However, the Culinary Delights from Around the World program will provide an excellent opportunity for nursing care residents to utilize their minds, to use their hands and to interact with fellow residents and community volunteers. Residents will learn new skills and information and will brush up on old skills. Residents will have an opportunity to share some of their own stories about their ethnic background, culture and favorite foods and recipes as the group discusses the various countries. The ability to reminisce about their lives should be a real stimulant and may help those who are homesick or who have lost their connection with their prior lives to reconnect to it. Residents will have an opportunity to have positive interaction with young people whom they may have been away from for a long time. The interaction will link two very different groups from two different eras who have different thoughts on life and living. The exchange of ideas could be mutually beneficial to both groups.

CONCLUSION

Recent research on geriatric issues has shown that facility-bound senior citizens need physical, visual, sensory and other types of stimulation. The recreational environment of nursing care facilities is sometimes sterile; opportunities for stimulation are sometimes extremely limited, for a variety of reasons.

Volunteerism is on the rise, and facilities should seek out ways to utilize the talents in the community. This, coupled with increasing numbers of school districts across the United States requiring volunteer commitments from students, makes this program a viable opportunity for senior citizens to expand their skills, to learn new skills and to engage in a healthful recreational activity and for students to make a worthwhile investment in the community. This program offers encouragement for our senior citizens and hope for our youth.

The Culinary Delights from Around the World program can be expanded to fit the needs of any nursing care facility and its residents. An abbreviated or expanded program may be implemented based on the needs of the residents and the resources available. What has been described here in these pages is a base program that serves as a guide. It is not intended to be limited or limiting. The success of the program hinges on the ability of the volunteer team and the nursing care facility staff to challenge, stimulate and revitalize the residents. This program will be exciting for everyone involved. The volunteer team will receive a great deal of satisfaction as they work to provide a whole wide world for the residents to see and to rediscover through food.

AUTHOR NOTE

Darlene J. Bruton received a Bachelor of General Studies, with a concentration in business administration and secondary education from the University of Maryland. She is President of the Bruton Group, a professional management consultant firm providing human resource development to for-profit and not-for-profit businesses.

Ms. Bruton has an extensive history with the aged and nursing homes. When employed with the National Capital Medical Foundation, she provided the administrative review for District of Columbia nursing home admissions.

REFERENCES

Bisignano, A. (1982). *Cooking the Italian Way.* Minneapolis: Lerner Publications Company.

Chung, O. and Monroe, J. (1988). *Cooking the Korean Way.* Minneapolis: Lerner Publications Company.

Munsen, S. (1982). *Cooking the Norwegian Way.* Minneapolis: Lerner Publications Company.

Parnell, H. (1991). *Cooking the South American Way.* Minneapolis: Lerner Publications Company.

Plotkin, G. and Plotkin, A. (1986). *Cooking the Russian Way.* Minneapolis: Lerner Publications Company.

Waldee, L. (1982). *Cooking the French Way.* Minneapolis: Lerner Publications Company.

Winget, M. (1991). *Desserts Around the World.* Minneapolis: Lerner Publications Company.

APPENDIX A

Desserts Around the World
SWEET BALLS (GHANA)–*Makes 20 to 25 doughnuts*
Recipe by Constance Nabwire and Bertha Vining Montgomery

1 egg
1/2 teaspoon salt
3 tablespoons baking powder
1 1/2 cups sugar
1/2 teaspoon nutmeg
1 1/2 cups warm water
3 3/4 to 4 1/4 cups all-purpose flour
vegetable oil

1. In a large bowl, combine egg, salt, baking powder, sugar and nutmeg, and stir well. Add 1 1/2 cups warm water and stir again.
2. Gradually stir in enough flour so that dough is stiff and only slightly sticky.
3. With clean, floured hands, roll dough into balls the size of walnuts.
4. Pour 1/2 inch oil into pan and heat over medium-high heat for 4 to 5 minutes.
5. Carefully place balls in oil, a few at a time, and fry 3 or 4 minutes per side or until golden brown. Remove from pan with slotted spoon and drain on paper towel. Serve warm.

Cooking the Korean Way
STEAMED CHICKEN WITH TOFU/Tubu tak kogi jjim–*Serves Four*
Recipe by Okwha Chung and Judy Monroe

1/3 cup soy sauce
3 tablespoons ketchup
1/8 teaspoon black pepper
1/8 teaspoon finely chopped ginger
1 clove garlic, peeled and crushed
1 green onion, finely chopped
3 to 4 medium carrots, peeled and cut into bite-size pieces
1/2 cup mushrooms, quartered
1/2 medium green pepper, seeded and cut into bite size pieces
6 chicken legs or thighs, skinned and boned, and cut into 1 1/2-inch pieces
1/2 cup tofu, drained and cut into 1-inch cubes (optional)

1. Combine all ingredients in a large heat-resistant bowl and mix well.
2. Pour 1/2 cup water into a steamer or large kettle and place bowl containing chicken mixture in water.
3. Bring water to a boil over high heat. Reduce heat to medium, cover pan, and steam for 20 to 25 minutes or until chicken is tender.
4. Serve hot with rice.

Cooking the Italian Way
BISIGNANO SPINACH/Spinaci Bisignano–*Serves Six to Eight*
Recipe by Alphonse Bisignano

2 10-ounce packages frozen chopped spinach, cooked, or 1 1/2 pounds
fresh spinach, cooked and finely chopped
1 16-ounce carton (2 cups) ricotta or cottage cheese
1 cup bread crumbs or packaged herb stuffing
2 eggs, lightly beaten
1/4 cup sliced fresh mushrooms or canned sliced mushrooms, drained
1/2 cup chopped green pepper
8 ounces (1 cup) sour cream
1/2 cup spaghetti sauce, canned or homemade
1 pound mozzarella cheese, sliced
1 teaspoon basil
1/2 cup grated Parmesan cheese

1. In a large bowl, combine spinach, ricotta or cottage cheese, bread crumbs, eggs, mushrooms, and green pepper.
2. Preheat the oven to 350 degrees.
3. Pour mixture into a buttered 9- by 13-inch baking dish and spread sour cream on top.
4. Pour on a layer of spaghetti sauce, using most but not all, of sauce. Cover with a layer of mozzarella cheese slices.
5. Spread remaining spaghetti sauce over cheese slices. Sprinkle with basil and Parmesan cheese.
6. Bake for 30 minutes.

Cooking the Norwegian Way
Potato Soup/Potetsuppe–*Serves Four*
Recipe by Sylvia Munsen

4 medium-sized potatoes
1 onion
1/2 teaspoon salt
2 cups whole milk
2 tablespoons butter
1/2 tablespoon chopped fresh parsley
1/8 teaspoon pepper

1. Peel each potato and cut into 4 pieces.
2. Peel onion and chop it well. Put potatoes, onion and salt in a heavy 2-quart saucepan. Pour water into the pan, covering vegetables.
3. Boil until a fork goes into potatoes easily (about 15 to 20 minutes). (Do not drain.) Then mash potatoes and onion in the pan.
4. Add milk slowly, stirring all the time. Allow soup to simmer while you add butter, parsley, and pepper.
5. Stir over medium heat until soup is smooth and hot.

Cooking the South American Way
MIXED GREEN SALAD/Ensalada Mixta–*Serves Six*
CHILE
Recipe by Helga Parnell

1 head Bibb lettuce
1 head romaine lettuce
4 ripe olives (optional)
4 cherry tomatoes, quartered (optional)
1/4 cup blue cheese, crumbled (optional)

1. Arrange lettuce in salad bowl.
2. Pour dressing over lettuce and toss to coat leaves. (See recipe below.)
3. Garnish with olives, tomatoes, and cheese.

Cooking the South American Way
DRESSING/Aliño–Makes about 1/2 cup
Recipe by Helga Parnell

1/2 cup olive oil
2 tablespoons lemon juice
1 large clove garlic, minced
1/2 teaspoon salt
1/4 teaspoon pepper

1. Combine all ingredients in a small jar.
2. Cover tightly and shake well.

Cooking the South American Way
FINGER SANDWICHES/Bocaditos
ARGENTINA
Recipe by Helga Parnell

12 thin slices French bread
1 3-ounce container whipped cream cheese with chives
1/2 cucumber, thinly sliced
4 to 6 precooked shrimps
4 cherry tomatoes
4 pimento-stuffed olives, sliced

1. Trim crusts from bread.
2. Spread a thin layer of cream cheese on bread.
3. Garnish with cucumber slices, a shrimp, cherry tomatoes, or olives.

Cooking the Russian Way
RASPBERRY KISEL/Malinoviy Kisel–*Serves Six*
Recipe by Gregory and Rita Plotkin

1 pound raspberries
1/2 cup cornstarch
8 1/2 cups water
1 cup sugar
whipped cream for topping

1. Wash raspberries in cold water and place in large bowl. Crush well with the back of a spoon. Set aside.
2. In a small bowl, combine cornstarch with 1/2 cup water and stir until cornstarch is completely dissolved. Set aside.
3. In a large saucepan, combine sugar and 8 cups of water and stir well. Bring to boil over high heat, stirring occasionally.
4. Add crushed fruit and cornstarch mixture to boiling syrup and stir until mixture begins to thicken.
5. Remove pan from heat and let *kisel* cool to room temperature before refrigerating. Serve chilled in glasses topped with whipped cream.

Cooking the Russian Way
HONEY SPICE CAKE/Kovrizhka Medovaya–Makes 9 to 12 pieces
Recipe by Gregory and Rita Plotkin

2 eggs
1/2 cup brown sugar
2 cups all-purpose flour
1/2 teaspoon baking soda
1 cup honey
1/2 cup raisins
1/2 cup sliced almonds (or other nuts)

1. Grease and flour a 9- by 5-inch loaf pan. Preheat oven to 350 degrees.
2. Beat eggs thoroughly in a small bowl.
3. Pour flour into a large mixing bowl. Add egg mixture and baking soda and stir well.
4. Add honey and mix for 10 minutes. Stir in raisins.
5. Pour dough into pan, level it out, and sprinkle with nuts.
6. Bake 50 to 60 minutes or until toothpick stuck in the middle of cake comes out clean.
7. Serve with whipped cream or jam.

Cooking the French Way
SALADE NICOISE–*Serves Four or Five*
Recipe by Lynne Marie Waldee

1 small head of lettuce
6 medium-sized cold cooked potatoes, sliced, or 1-pound can small
  whole white potatoes
1/2 pound fresh green beans or 1 10-ounce package frozen green beans,
  cooked, cold, and cut into 1/2 inch lengths
1/2 cup vinaigrette dressing (See recipe below.)
 1 13-ounce can tuna, drained (optional)
black or green olives for garnish (optional)

1. Wash and separate lettuce leaves, throwing away any that are wilted or discolored. Arrange leaves decoratively in a large, shallow serving plate and set aside.
2. In a large mixing bowl, combine potatoes, beans, and tomatoes. Pour vinaigrette dressing over vegetables. Using 2 spoons, carefully toss vegetables until they are thoroughly coated.
3. Spoon vegetables onto lettuce leaves and top with mound of tuna and/or olives.

Cooking the French Way
VINAIGRETTE DRESSING/Vinaigrette–*Enough for 4 or 5 salad*
servings
Recipe by Lynne Marie Waldee

1 clove garlic
1 teaspoon salt
3 tablespoons red wine vinegar
1/4 teaspoon pepper
 6 tablespoons olive or vegetable oil

1. Chop garlic into very fine pieces and put in a small bowl.
2. Use the back of a spoon to mash garlic. Then mix it with salt.
3. Add vinegar and pepper, stirring until smooth.
4. Place in a small jar with a tight-fitting lid. Add oil, screw on lid, and shake until well blended.

Gardening–
An Equal Opportunity Joy

Pamela L. McKee

SUMMARY. The rich colors poured out of flowers can serve as a soothing balm during periods of grief and loneliness. The care and keeping of an indoor garden can be the motivator for the homebound or physically challenged person whose mobility limits full participation in an outdoor garden. More importantly, however, a garden can serve as a catalyst for social sharing among members of a community and enrich the lives of each participant in a very special way. *[Article copies available from The Haworth Document Delivery Service: 1-800-342-9678.]*

The garden holds wonderful and powerful gifts for each individual irrespective of age, class and circumstance; it's an equal opportunity joy for males and females and is not limited by language proficiency or available space. A prospective participant may begin a garden in flower pots hung around porches or balconies, window boxes placed on selected window sills, a designated area to the front or back of one's home, a special spot lobbied for on behalf of residents in an apartment building, or a subplot in a large community garden in the neighborhood.

The joy of gardening is not limited to one's expertise or past educational feats. The gardener is accepted at any stage, whether that person is a

Pamela L. McKee is a Program Development Consultant in Washington, DC.
Address correspondence to the author at: 431 Oneida Place, N.W., Washington, DC, 20011.
The author thanks her neighbors, many of whom are members of the "golden generation."

[Haworth co-indexing entry note]: "Gardening–An Equal Opportunity Joy," McKee, Pamela L. Co-published simultaneously in *Activities, Adaptation & Aging* (The Haworth Press, Inc.) Vol. 20, No. 1, 1995, pp. 71-78; and: *Volunteerism in Geriatric Settings* (ed: Vera R. Jackson), The Haworth Press, Inc., 1995, pp. 71-78. Single or multiple copies of this article/chapter may be purchased from The Haworth Document Delivery Center [1-800-342-9678, 9:00 a.m. - 5:00 p.m. (EST)].

stumbling novice or a seasoned expert. The area of concentration is guided only by one's personal taste which may range from herbs, vegetables, annual or perennial flowers, or shrubberies and trees. There are many intergenerational stories which can be told and histories shared, while nurturing one's favorite flowers or vegetables.

AN INTERGENERATIONAL COMMUNITY AFFAIR

The organization that incorporates a gardening program into its senior activities program may choose to involve its participants at any level, dependent upon their physical or mental capacities and the size of the garden available. Physically challenged residents in an apartment building may watch the blooms from the window sill or encourage the bulbs to burst forth from a dirt-filled bowl right within the room. Some participants may elect to organize community groups and choose to plant a large flower or vegetable garden in the open areas designated for such uses by various governments in cities across the nation. Smaller groups within community residential facilities or larger retirement communities may work with resident managers and the maintenance support staff to improve their surroundings, while they simultaneously receive the benefits of recreation and socialization.

A telephone reassurance program may be designed around the sharing of indoor plants maintained by a senior citizen and a community volunteer. While caring for the plants, the senior citizen and volunteer could develop a trusting relationship that might enable each of them to openly discuss a number of topics including those related to major life events such as health and death.

Members of a senior program who live in the same neighborhood and enjoy their own homes may join together and request free trees from projects sponsored annually by various government agencies and nonprofit organizations. In some major metropolitan areas, the local governments participate in the environmental thrust and beautification of the inner cities by making free shrubberies and trees available to its residents on a first-come, first-served basis.

Garden clubs may be organized among participants in large retirement housing communities. Some of the activities for these clubs may include educational winter research programs designed around videos shown on vegetables, plants, herbs, and trees. These clubs may also include site visits to annual flower shows at convention centers and the seasonal highlights of well-known gardens which begin in late March through October. There are also wide opportunities available for many plant nurseries to participate in their communities through their annual donations to beautification projects along the many streets inhabited by senior citizens where the annual planting event incorporates the students from neighborhood schools.

THE SPIRITUAL MEDICINE OF COLOR

There are few individuals who would hesitate to confess to the healing power of color. Many flower shop owners do brisk business during the flu season because flowers tend to have a warm soothing effect. The range of colors inherent in flowers speak to us of a universal power much greater than man, whether we gaze into the "heart" of a yellow tulip or the "soul" of a deep purple bearded Japanese iris. It is difficult to continue to believe that true and infinite power begins and ends with each of us as we inhale the bold fragrance of the blood-red mirandy rose, the delicate fragrance held in a pink hyacinth, or the fragile scent secured in the white bell-shaped flowers of the lily of the valley.

The care givers, friends, and associates of older persons understand that many individuals in this population are frequently challenged with grief and depression brought on, in many instances, by the death of a child, spouse, childhood friend, or significant other. The smorgasbord of colors seen in flowers and gardens as they burst forth with life can serve as the best medicine for uplifting the spirit and mood of those encouraged to participate in planting and nurturing flowers. There is powerful rejuvenation of mood and spirit that is granted to the individual who is welcomed into a room by a vase of freshly-cut mixed blooms of tulips and daffodils, or a cluster of red, pink and yellow roses highlighted by the fragile strength shown in several deep purple Japanese irises, or the graceful beauty of the long-stemmed orange day lilies.

The stubborn and persistent challenge of aches and pains during the winter may suddenly take leave once a hoe, rake or shovel is taken in hand and the weeds in the community plot are tamed by the physical exercise of joints which are now being exercised during the spring or summer. The emotional burdens of grief unexpressed and tears unshed, over the loss of a friend or loved one, may now be salved by the foot that presses firmly against that shovel as one digs a hole to receive a tree that is to be planted in memory of that loved one. In the months and years ahead, the healing juices could flow through the energies given to the weeding, mulching and fertilizing, and the "discussions" with that tree to urge it to demonstrate life and to bloom in honor of the "energetic spirit" of the loved one who may have passed away recently.

PROFILE OF A PORTABLE
RESIDENTIAL COMMUNITY GARDEN

The following model is geared towards a senior residential facility or retirement community which allows residents to participate in the development of the surroundings. Residents and staff may join together to lobby the management for a designated area for this project. The design incorporates those residents who would like to participate, but because of physical challenges, may not be able to join the group for outside activities and, therefore, would maintain their gardens on the inside of their apartments or on balconies.

The volunteer body for this project would be recruited from among the students in the neighboring schools. Plants and other equipment could be solicited from nurseries, hardware stores and from the neighborhood at large (see sample letters). The thrust of the design of this indoor/outdoor portable garden would emphasize year round blooms and a wealth of color to be enjoyed by residents, family members, and volunteers. The portability allows for indoor gardeners to take their prized possessions to "visit" the outdoor garden for short or long periods of time and support social interaction among the two groups of gardeners and volunteers. A special annual spring or summer event may be developed around the initial "coming out" of the indoor delights, their owners/protectors and telephone reassurance volunteer plant care givers.

Since we recognize that we live in an imperfect world, it should not be hard to believe that there are some individuals who consciously choose not to enjoy flowers or are unable to enjoy the marvelous blooms because of medical challenges such as allergies. These individuals may, however, elect to participate in gardening through maintaining an herb garden. Many herbs may be purchased as young plants and directions for planting followed carefully. Selections for an herb garden offers broadleaf sage, nasturtium, sweet basil, french and spanish thyme, chives, rosemary, curled parsley, and french tarragon and many of these plants may be combined in a clay, redwood or concrete pot, or in window boxes.

HELP IS AVAILABLE ALL AROUND US

There are large bodies of helpers in our schools, churches, and on military bases. Many strong, able-bodied young men and women from the

Army or Navy would welcome the opportunity to be of assistance digging the dirt and doing other initial heavy-duty gardening chores for a particular nursing home or community residence for senior citizens. Similarly, many large nurseries would consider donating plants and seeds each spring. Hardware stores may consider donating small and bulky gardening tools which once received, may be kept for many years. Mr. and Mrs. John Q. Public would embrace the opportunity to contribute one bag of peat moss, mulch or other gardening accessories on a regular basis, each year, if they are not inclined to be a part of the volunteer body who work in other areas. The same applies for the garden pots and other containers which may be either solicited from the community at large or purchased from funds raised through the annual sales of arts and crafts or baked goods.

Any project that is approached with enthusiasm and the full belief that it can be converted into a community affair brings to it myriad possibilities to be seized and benefits to be gained. Our neighborhoods serve as temporary and permanent hosts to hundreds of individuals who would elect to become a part of them once they are invited to participate.

The attached sample letters are guides to fostering enthusiasm and the "yes we can" spirit which are limited only by our thinking and lack of will to make a difference in enriching the lives of our senior citizens. You are cordially invited to respond to the call of the earth, that is echoed in the vast array of containers, as it shouts: "Let's do it"!

AUTHOR NOTE

Pamela L. McKee completed a BS degree in Psychology and MA in Education Administration at Howard University. Since moving to the United States in 1969, she has served in various capacities including Special Assistant for Administration during the Carter Administration, President and Manager of her own retail business for six years and Executive Director of a large social service agency. She is currently a Program Development Consultant using her experience in aging, mental health, economic development and youth services to serve both public and private organizations.

Ms. McKee is an alumni of Leadership Washington, Class of 1994; board member, District of Columbia Chamber of Commerce; board member, Casa Iris; member, Women of Washington; and member, National Association of Female Executives.

REFERENCES

Glattstein, Judith. *The American Gardener's World of Bulbs (Bulbs for Formal and Informal Gardens.* New York: Little, Brown and Company, 1994.
Gardening in Containers. California: Lane Publishing Co. Menlo Park, 1977.

Hathaway, Polly. *The Beginning Knowledge Book of Backyard Flowers*. Ruthledge Books, Inc., 1965.

Schuler, Stanley. *The Gardener's Basic Book of Flowers. A Guide to Best Small Flowering Plants–Annuals, Perennials, Bulbs and Roses*. New York: Simon and Schuster, 1974.

Scott-James, Ann. *Perfect Plant, Perfect Garden. The 200 Most Rewarding Plants for Every Garden*. New York: Summit Books, 1988.

Simpson, Norman. *The Complete Plant Doctor. The Instant Guide to Health Indoor Bulbs and Annuals*, edited by David Longman. New York: Times Books, Random House, Inc., 1985.

Taloumis, George. *Container Gardening Outdoors*. New York: Simon and Schuster, 1972.

Taylor, Norman. *Taylor's Guide to Bulbs*, edited by Gordon P. DeWolf, Jr. New York: Houghton Miflin Company, 1986.

Taylor, Norman. *Taylor's Guide to Annuals*, edited by Gordon P. DeWolf, Jr. New York: Houghton Miflin Company, 1986.

Taylor, Norman. *Taylor's Guide to Houseplants*, edited by Gordon P. DeWolf, Jr. New York: Houghton Miflin Company, 1987.

Taylor, Norman. *Taylor's Guide to Roses*, edited by Gordon P. by DeWolf, Jr. New York: Houghton Miflin Company, 1986.

Taylor, Patricia A. *Easy Care Shade Flowers How to Plan and Cultivate a Colorful Environment-Friendly Shade Garden with Practically No Maintenance*. Fireside: Simon and Schuster, 1993.

The editors of Garden Way Publishing (with foreword by Henry W. Art). *Annuals: 1001 Gardening Questions Answered*. New Jersey: Doubleday Book and Music Clubs, Inc., 1989.

The United States National Arboretum, Program Aid Number 309, prepared by Agricultural Research Service. Washington, D.C.: revised May 1986; slightly revised January 1991.

The Washington Post. Washington Home Magazine, Spring Garden Issue, March 23, 1995.

APPENDIX

XYZ RESIDENTIAL FACILITY
1234 JOY AVENUE
UNITED STATES OF AMERICA

Date_____

Mr. Miracle Worker
President
Community Neighborhood Hardware
5678 Yes We Want to Help Avenue
United States of America

Dear _____:

The XYZ Residential Facility is home to more than two hundred and twenty residents ranging in ages from 65 to 92 years. Many of our residents continue to be active and involved in a wide range of hobbies including travelling abroad, photography, arts and crafts and gardening.

This year, twenty of these residents have agreed to form the "Frisky Garden Club" and embark upon planting a small area at the entrance of the building. Once completed, the garden would serve as nature's member on the "Warm Welcome Committee" to visitors, as well as a place for our residents to stretch, exercise and enjoy the beauty and joy of colorful flowers during the spring and summer.

Please join us in making this a special project for the physical, mental and psychological well being of our excited residents by donating the following:

_____

(always state your needs)

The enclosed brochure is provided to give you some additional information on XYZ. We appreciate your generosity toward the success of this exciting community project and, of course, look forward to seeing you or your designated representative next spring when the garden will be opened to the public for viewing.

Sincerely,

_____

Director, Resident Activities Services

P.S.: Your contributions would be used by our volunteer body from John and Mary Junior High School in our neighborhood.

Enclosure

XYZ RESIDENTIAL FACILITY
1234 JOY AVENUE
UNITED STATES OF AMERICA

Date_____

Commanding Officer
ROTC
John and Mary Junior High School
5678 Avenue of the Students
United States of America

Dear _____:

The XYZ Residential Facility is home to more than two hundred and twenty residents ranging in age from 65 to 92 years. Many of our residents continue to be active and involved in a wide range of hobbies including travelling abroad, photography, arts and crafts and gardening.

This year, twenty of these residents have agreed to form the "Frisky Garden Club" and embark upon planting a small area at the entrance of the building. Once completed, the garden would serve as nature's member on the "Warm Welcome Committee" to visitors, as well as a place for our residents to stretch, exercise and enjoy the beauty and joy of colorful flowers during the spring and summer.

We are extending a special invitation to the young men and women of the ROTC to join us as volunteers in making this a special project for the physical, mental and psychological well being of our excited residents. The time commitment is minimal–4 hours each week; 2 hours each Wednesday and Saturday–beginning April 1 through May 31. The students would assist the residents in preparing the area and planting the flowers. Some of these students and their parents may wish to serve as telephone reassurance nursery guides for the indoor gardeners. This aspect of our unique intergenerational project would assist residents with the care and nurturing of the plants of their choice.

The enclosed brochure is provided to give you some additional information on XYZ. We appreciate your generosity toward the success of this exciting community project and, of course, look forward to seeing you, the ROTC members and parents next spring, when the garden will be opened to the public for viewing.

Sincerely,

_____

Director, Resident Activities Services

Enclosure

Volunteering to Promote Fitness and Caring:
A Motive for Linking College Students with Mature Adults

Ladd Colston
Shirley Harper
Wanda Mitchener-Colston

SUMMARY. This article will investigate and describe efforts to use college students as volunteers with mature adults. The fitness trend has encouraged people, both young and old, to actively participate in appropriate physical and recreation activities. A common desire for both longevity and quality of life are discussed as a means for linking college students with mature adults on college campuses and in geriatric service settings. Achieving fitness through one's participation in sport and exercise programs has become synonymous with good health. Short term benefits often cited include a positive impact on hypertension, osteoporosis, general well-being, self-concept, self-esteem, psychological mood, muscular strength, endurance and social integration. Studies on the effectiveness of intergenerational contact have fostered favorable images and attitudes towards older

Ladd Colston, PhD, is Associate Professor at Old Dominion University in Norfolk, VA. Shirley Harper, PhD, is Assistant Professor at North Carolina Central University in Durham, NC. Wanda Mitchener-Colston, PhD, is Assistant Dean in the College of Arts and Letters at Norfolk State University in Norfolk, VA.

[Haworth co-indexing entry note]: "Volunteering to Promote Fitness and Caring: A Motive for Linking College Students with Mature Adults,"Colston, Ladd, Shirley Harper, and Wanda Mitchener-Colston. Co-published simultaneously in *Activities, Adaptation & Aging* (The Haworth Press, Inc.) Vol. 20, No. 1, 1995, pp. 79-90; and: *Volunteerism in Geriatric Settings* (ed: Vera R. Jackson), The Haworth Press, Inc., 1995, pp. 79-90. Single or multiple copies of this article/chapter may be purchased from The Haworth Document Delivery Center [1-800-342-9678, 9:00 a.m. - 5:00 p.m. (EST)].

persons by younger persons. As a direct result, there is encouraging evidence to support the value of college students volunteering to actively participate alongside mature adults in fitness programs. Motives for involvement are discussed relative to college students understanding the importance of caring as citizenship and the application of volunteer experiences to professional career pursuits. Caring is discussed as a rising social need which has increased in demand by middle-aged persons, or the middle generation, who must now independently care for their aging children, their aging parents and their aging grandparents. Suggestions for program development are recommended for college campuses. *[Article copies available from The Haworth Document Delivery Service: 1-800-342-9678.]*

Volunteerism is on the decline. A lack of time and a disregard for *caring as citizenship* are now characteristic of the majority of American citizens today. According to Juliet Schor (1994), the time squeeze has taken its toll on volunteer activities. Most people do not have the time to care for themselves, much less others. People are working longer hours and stress is now a major influence on what people are willing to do during their leisure time.

Serving and caring for others was once an accepted responsibility of all American citizens. It was a function of "citizenship," a term that is rarely used today. Fitch (1987) found that volunteerism is influenced at an early age. Major influences come from friends (40%), followed closely by parents (33%). Others involved include teachers (8%), public figures (4%), siblings (3%), religious leaders (3%) and no influence (9%). People now tend to be self-serving and dominated by a need to fulfill self-interests. Today, adults have little time to volunteer or to care for others and as a direct result are raising a generation of non-caring children. These children will in turn not understand the need or obligation to give back to their community. College students are individuals who are preparing themselves for professional career pursuits and many are in a position to comprehend the importance of becoming socially responsible. The value of volunteerism can be taught in the college community, but there are a number of critical factors that must be understood if any efforts are to prove successful.

Volunteering encompasses meeting people, gaining knowledge from people and acquiring insight and personal satisfaction. Volunteer work has often been referred to as the secret to happiness–the immeasurable reward that comes from serving others. A devotion to serving and caring for others can be interpreted as recreation that is self-satisfying. It characterizes the "learning lifestyle" that is discussed by Ken Dychtwald (1989) in his landmark text entitled *Age Wave*. College students are in a position of *gaining* knowledge, whereas mature adults are in a position of *sharing* knowledge. It appears that this dichotomy needs to be utilized as a prime opportunity to promote volunteerism through intergenerational programs and services.

A public commitment to good health and longevity has caused an explosion in the fitness and wellness movements. Economically, the National Sporting Goods Association (1994) has produced data that reflects a consistent rise in consumer purchasing of fitness clothing and equipment by persons ages 45 to 64 years. Fitness, exercise and recreation have the potential to improve the health and quality of life for all ages, including today's and tomorrow's older adults. Physical fitness can develop efficiency of heart and lungs, muscular strength, endurance, balance, flexibility, coordination and agility which in turn can enable people of all ages to live life vigorously, energetically and healthfully. Exercise can be found to lower blood pressure, decrease the percentage of body fat, increase maximum oxygen intake and improve arm strength. Leisure activity can reduce stress, develop social interaction, increase psychological well-being and facilitate one's enjoyment of life.

Ideally, preparation for lifelong fitness should begin during young adulthood in order that maximum benefits accrue. Documented research (deVries, 1985; Shepard; 1978; and Smith, 1981) has demonstrated the benefits of exercise to people of all ages, especially those who undertake a program of regular progressive, sensible, physical exercise, individually prescribed to meet each person's fitness requirements. Past studies have shown a startling difference between active and inactive seniors. Active seniors show an increase in vitality, less dependence on laxatives, fewer visits to the physician and improved general functioning. Inactive seniors, on the other hand, show an increase in prescription medications, susceptibility to illness, loneliness, depression, and suicide.

Volunteerism has most often involved retired persons who have large amounts of discretionary time and are willing to devote it to helping others. Due to the increase of mature adults who are living longer, alone and without families or friends, the demand for volunteers outweighs the supply. According to Brody (1985), more adult children are involved in caring for frail parents and grandparents, to the point that parent care is now a normative experience for adult children. The percentage of middle aged adults who have always been the dominant supplier of volunteers in hospitals, senior centers, churches and schools has declined. Low numbers of men, ethnic group members and low income persons continues to be visibly apparent in settings outside the family and the church. Volunteerism for mature adults is slowly evolving into a growing crisis.

This article will explore the idea of attracting college students to volunteer with mature adults by examining common motives and facilitating mutual needs. Leisure and fitness are two forms of activity that facilitate participatory competence, self-esteem and social relationships. It is felt that college students represent a prime population to pursue for developing mutually beneficial volunteer opportunities.

STUDENT LEARNING THROUGH INVOLVEMENT

Little research has been done specifically on how to motivate college student involvement in community service. Fitch (1987) found that motivation for volunteering can be divided into three categories: (1) *altruistic* where the goal is to increase others' welfare (i.e., I am concerned about those less fortunate than me.), (2) *egoistic* where the goal is to increase the helper's welfare (i.e., It gives me a good feeling or sense of satisfaction to help others.), and (3) *social obligation* where the goal is to repay a debt to society (i.e., I would hope that someone would help me or my family if I were in a similar situation.). Of the three, the egoistic category was the most popular forum for motivating college students to perform community service. This finding appears to indicate the importance of self-interest in volunteer activities. Egoistic rewards are necessary and their importance may be the key to increasing the quantity and quality of college student involvement. Phillips (1982) found that students can be enticed to participate using a variety of reward systems and "if a quality experience is offered, the goal of increasing humanitarian concern and civil responsibility (caring and citizenship) will follow."

At the University of West Florida, Redfering and Biasco (1982) developed a program in which psychology students were able to volunteer for college credit. The program provided students with an opportunity to practically apply what they were learning in psychology as well as to gain experience in the real world. The authors found that students were more willing to participate in volunteer efforts for academic credit than for recognition or money. To remove the anxiety and inflation of grades, a "pass" or "fail" grading system was instituted for the course. This program could be considered as a predecessor of the field-based practicum or senior internship that is found in many courses of study today. Nevertheless, the point remains that one should consider integrating the value of service into the total college experience and reinforce its presence with an egoistic reward.

Motivation, by definition, is an abstract psychological construct, whereas involvement is active in a behavioral sense. In his landmark article on student involvement, Astin (1984) postulated that " the amount of student learning and personal involvement associated with any educational program is directly proportional to the quantity and quality of student involvement in that program." Involvement here implies a behavioral component. It can be susceptible to direct observation and measurement. As Astin goes on to say "It is not so much what the individual thinks or feels, but what the individual does, how he or she behaves, that defines and identifies involvement." Student involvement can include one's absorption in academic work, one's participation in extracurricular activities and/or one's interaction with faculty and other institutional personnel. According to Astin (1984), the greater the student's involvement in college, the greater will be the amount of student learning and personal development.

Boyer (1990) encourages colleges to examine campus life and how a strong learning community can evolve from a balance of individual student interests and shared university concerns (i.e., crime, prejudice, commitment to academic life). Boyer goes on to say that a caring community could promote the opportunity for students to not only meet their educational needs, but also prepare themselves for their social and civic responsibilities. In specific, Cooper, Healy and Simpson (1994) recommend that the work of the student affairs office on college campuses encompass not only the needs of individual students and students in groups, but must also create campus cultures that promote student involvement in the community.

THE INTERGENERATIONAL GOAL OF FITNESS

Dietary and physical activity patterns are associated with five of the 10 leading causes of death in the United States including: coronary heart disease, some cancers, stroke, non-insulin-dependent diabetes mellitus and atherosclerosis. Physical activity can contribute vastly to overall health and an improved quality of life. Among those aged 65 years and over, the percentage reporting regular exercise rose from 29% in 1985 to 32% in 1990. It is important that aging adults recognize early the effect of fitness on physical and mental well-being.

Research by Havighurst (1963) basically assumed that older people who are active will be more satisfied and better adjusted than less active older people. This activity perspective is perhaps most strikingly apparent in the numerous recreation and fitness programs sponsored by retirement communities and senior centers to attract new clientele. The Second Duke Longitudinal Study (Palmore, 1979) found that being involved in physical activity was a major predictor of "successful aging." Exercise of moderate intensity was found to benefit aging participants by improving cardiovascular status, decreasing fracture risk, increasing functional ability, and improving mental processing.

In many cases, the attitudes expressed by mature adults toward fitness and exercise pose major barriers in program development. Barriers include the common myth that the older one gets, the less need there is for exercise. In addition, negative attitudes reinforce the feeling that their abilities are limited and exercise might be dangerous. Conrad (1977) found that these barriers can inhibit active participation in fitness programs. However, with creative program development and effective management strategies, these barriers can be overcome. This article proposes the implementation of intergenerational fitness programs utilizing college students. It is strongly felt that current trends in activity research support the merit of forging a partnership between college students and mature adults within a common focus.

An intergenerational fitness program could sensitize the college student to his/her attitudes toward aging and the aging process, as well as the critical importance of caring through volunteerism. According to Angelis (1992), intergenerational fitness programs should be a three-way partnership of college students, mature adults and academic institutions. All must cooperate in order to provide a mutually effective program. Overall, the outcomes of an intergenerational fitness program utilizing college students as volunteers should be to: (1) positively affect the physical well-being of participating mature adults, (2) provide an opportunity for mature adults (65 years and over) to participate in a leisure and fitness program which can improve their quality of life, and (3) provide an opportunity for students to learn about the aging process and history. A by-product of this intergenerational fitness program could result in a collaborative model of service delivery in leisure and fitness for older Americans.

An intergenerational fitness program could also sensitize the college student to his/her attitudes toward aging and transform these attitudes into an understanding of the aging process and the caring role required of citizens and professionals in providing services to the aging. The value of practical experience is an important component of an educational program for college students. Studies and classroom interactions, while valid elements of the total academic experience are not sufficient in and of themselves to prepare students for citizenship. Fitch (1990) found that college student volunteers involved in community service activities were ranked high in reference to interpersonal values and independence when compared to other college students. Students must have the opportunity to implement the substance of preparatory programs in an environment consistent with the settings in which they will work. Students, by participating in an intergenerational fitness program on campus or in geriatric settings, could (1) improve the educational process, (2) have a laboratory for application of theoretical knowledge, and thereby (3) enable the faculty to assess the quality and relevance of coursework more effectively. Most students will find intergenerational fitness programs rewarding. Many will develop an understanding of aging and be able to effectively present a more accurate and balanced view of aging. Some students will foster respect and admiration of their aging classmates. Mature adults can also benefit from intergenerational contact with college students in a fitness program. Mature adults can improve their physical fitness, share learned skills, increase life satisfaction, and expand their social contacts.

Strategies for program planning and development of an intergenerational fitness program should include the following six (6) components: (1) *A Needs Assessment*, which includes defining what is expected to be accomplished from the mature adult and the college student's perspectives; (2) *Reachable Goals and Objectives*, which are result-oriented and will benefit both the college student and the mature adult; (3) *Volunteer Role Descriptions*, which will initially inform college student volunteers as to the purpose of the program, what skills are necessary, the amount of time commitment to anticipate, and what is expected of them; (4) *Orientation and Training*, which should be designed to inform both mature adult and college student of the physical, mental, social and emotional needs characteristic of their respective stages in the life cycle as well as their environmental influences; (5) *Program Monitoring*, which should examine whether activities employed in the program are meeting the needs expressed by participants in the Needs Assessment; and (6) *Program Evaluation*, which should formally determine whether the Reachable Goals and Objectives of the program have been achieved. It is felt by the authors that a critical facilitator of these strategies will be open and honest communications, which must be consistently employed between mature adult, college student and program leader(s). Oftentimes, the lack of interpersonal communications can lead to participant dissatisfaction and confusion amongst activity leaders and volunteers.

Program and policy measures can develop from intergenerational fitness programs that could help close the gap between college students and mature adults, simultaneously advancing mature adult services-college student development and intergenerational cooperation. Involvement in community service can also benefit college student volunteers by helping them feel valued and foster development of civic/community responsibility.

Involvement in physical activity is regarded as an important influence on health and fitness of all age groups. Research has shown that well-being has been most strongly related to physical health and degree of social interaction for mature adults. Development and management of an effective volunteer fitness program involving college students and mature adults can offer new, beneficial and unique perspectives to the generation gap.

VOLUNTEERISM AS A LEISURE ALTERNATIVE

Community service needs to be defined as a "leisure alternative" rather than a way to work. Defined in this way, some college students can be attracted by the chance to engage in a contributory form of leisure that brings pleasure, not drudgery. Short term, semester or seasonal, volunteer assignments could help encourage college students to respond favorably to a perceived community need. Aging populations of over one million in California, New York, Florida, Pennsylvania, Texas, Illinois, Ohio, Michigan, and New Jersey could benefit from a positive surge in college student volunteerism. National efforts to attract college students to volunteer with America's mature adults should include the following strategies: (1) change the public image of old age and the elderly, (2) redefine the nature and merits of volunteerism, and (3) expand opportunities to volunteer in existing organizations. As was noted earlier, students can be enticed to participate using a variety of reward systems. Fitness and sport are popular participatory activities that entail perceived benefits such as increased endurance, muscle strength, weight loss, physical attraction, and longevity. Both young and old can find pleasure in active participation in these activities. The college campus represents home for the college student and for the mature adult, it can represent a learning environment that is both stimulating and young at heart.

The experiential meaning of leisure is important and must be related to developmental and social meanings. According to Lawton (1993), the meaning of leisure activities in the lives of mature adults can be categorized as (1) *experiential,* involving intrinsic satisfaction in the activity itself, solitude, diversion, and relaxation; (2) *developmental,* involving intellectual challenge, personal competence, expression, personal development, and creativity; and (3) *social,* involving social interaction, social status, and service. A balanced mix of physical activity and stimulating recreation can be integral to promoting preventive health and a meaningful lifestyle in mature adults. Current research (Tedrick, 1991) substantiates the fact that there is a strong correlation between leisure participation and life satisfaction in mature adults. Intergenerational programs involving mature adults must incorporate the element of leisure participation, preferably physical activity, which can offer the anticipated outcomes of life satisfaction and quality of life.

Modifications in work patterns and organizational opportunities for career development are changing the definition of leisure. Job sharing, sabbaticals, lifelong education and phased retirement reinforce this current trend by projecting a "blurring" of work and leisure related activities. Increased organizational awareness of employee needs, such as on-the-job exercise and fitness programs, child care, staff training and psychological counseling reflect a more balanced view of work and leisure in society. Therefore, it is not unrealistic to expect that the youth of today, or the future mature adults of tomorrow, will view leisure in retirement as a continuation of their leisure activities during their younger years and will not regard it as a new stage of life. The traditional linear life cycle of education for the young, employment for the middle aged, and retirement for the old are already undergoing major changes. In 1985, more than 45 percent of college students were over age 25, while the average age of community college students was 38 (Dychtwald and Flower, 1989).

The interdependence of generations across the life span can be instrumental in providing for future policy and program development. Intergenerational programs can utilize the experiences and developed skills of the mature adult to provide children and youth with opportunities to interact and learn. University campuses, schools, community centers, nursing homes, retirement facilities and adult day care centers can offer cooperative, cross-age efforts that can reduce ageism and competition among age groups.

DISCUSSION

Trends in divorce and remarriage are reshaping the life course and social networks of young and old. A growing number of children, parents and grandparents can devote substantial effort toward building reconstituted families and steprelationships, only to find them eventually dissolved (Hooyman and Kiyak, 1993). Divorced fathers, for example, are less likely to keep in touch with their children or to name them as a source of support. Patterns of support are disrupted by divorce, remarriage and redivorce. It is estimated that more than 30 percent of all children under age 16 will experience the divorce of their parents. In addition, the loss of parents is not expected until the second half of adulthood, and the death of a child is no longer an anticipated part of family life. As a direct result, increased life expectancy means that more adult children will have to care for frail parents and grandparents. Combined with reduced fertility, adult children can expect to spend more years caring for aging parents than their dependent children.

Young and old need to work together in order to benefit the needy in our society. As the aging population continues to increase, the decisions regarding the allocation of health care to individuals will assume greater importance. These decisions will have to be made by an informed and humanistic society. To make informed choices, today's youth will have to understand the processes of aging, as well as the policies and services that affect the aging population. Currently, long term care for a chronic illness or functional limitation represents the most devastating threat to economic security of most Americans. According to Hooyman and Kiyak (1993), if disability rates remain constant, the number of mature adults needing assistance will double between 1990 and 2030, and the number of mature adults requiring nursing home care will more than triple.

The expectation that families should and will assume more responsibility for long term care is unrealistic. Women, the traditional supply of caregivers for the aging, will not volunteer as in the past due to their increased movement into the workforce and the subsequent demands of full-time and career employment. In fact, women and persons of color will account for over 60 percent of the projected labor force by the year 2000. Diminishing resources and the growing number of uninsured chronically ill will challenge the social value placed on our aging citizenry. What will be the obligation of the young to care for the old in the face of health care needs and the rising costs of human welfare? What better way to address these issues and concerns than to provide college students with an opportunity for learning, awareness, dialogue and understanding through volunteerism? What better way to provide an open forum for mature adults to actively discuss the benefits of preventive health and their legacy to the future than to provide an intergenerational fitness program designed for mutual enjoyment and interaction?

REFERENCES

Altman, Janice and Sedlacek, William. (1990). *Differences in volunteer interest by level of career orientation. Research Report #5-90.* College Park, MD: Counseling Center, University of Maryland.

Angelis, Jane. (1992). The genesis of an intergenerational program. *Educational Gerontology*, 18, (4), 317-327.

Astin, Alexander W. (1984). Student involvement: A developmental theory for higher education. *Journal of College Student Personnel*, 25 (4), 297-308.

Bortz, W.M. (1992). Disuse and aging. *Journal of the American Medical Association*, 248, 1203-1208.

Boyer, E. (1990). *Campus Life.* Princeton, NJ: The Carnegie Foundation for the Advancement of Teaching.

Brody, E. (1985). Parent care as a normative family stress. *The Gerontologist*, 25 (1), 19-30.

Clements, Claire B. (1994). *The arts/fitness quality of life activities program: creative ideas for working with older adults in group settings.* Baltimore, MD: Health Professions Press.

Collison, Michelle. (1989). For some students, Spring break offers chance to aid the needy. *Chronicle of Higher Education*, 35 (28), 33-34.

Cooper, D., Healy, M., and Simpson, J. (1994). Student development through involvement: Specific changes over time. *Journal of College Student Personnel*, 35 (2), 98-102.

deVries, H.A. (1985). Physiological effects of an exercise training regimen on men ages 52-99. *Journal of Gerontology*, 25, 325-336.

Duggar, Margaret L. (1993). *Intergenerational programs: weaving hearts and minds.* Tallahassee, Florida: Florida Council on Aging, Florida State Department of Education.

Dychtwald, Ken. (1989). *Age Wave: The Challenges and Opportunities of an Aging America.* Los Angeles, CA: Jeremy P. Tarcher, Inc.

Fitch, R.T. (1987). Characteristics and motivations of college students volunteering for community service. *Journal of College Student Personnel*, 28 (5), 424-431.

Fitch, R.T. (1990). Differences in interpersonal values among students involved in volunteer service. *College Student Affairs Journal*, 10 (1), 36-42.

Fox. Susan and Giles, Howard. (1993). Accommodating intergenerational contact: a critique and theoretical model. *Journal of Aging Studies*, 7 (4), 423-451.

Greenberg, Jerrold and Dintiman, George. (1991). *College student self-care diary.* Reston, VA: AAHPERD Publications.

Havinghurst, R.J. (1963). Successful aging. In R. Williams, C. Tibbits, and W. Donahue (eds.) *Process of aging (Vol.1).* New York: Atherton Press.

Hooyman, N. R. and Kiyak, H.A. (1993). *Social Gerontology. Third Edition.* Needham Heights, Massachusetts: Allyn and Bacon.

Kelly, John R., Ed. (1993). *Activity and Aging: Staying involved in later life.* Sage Focus Editions, Vol. 161. Thousand Oaks, CA: Sage Publications.

Morrisey, A. M. (1991). Student activities: Focus on strengthening community through involvement. *Campus Activities Programming*, 24 (6), 45-53.

National Sporting Goods Association. (1994). *Sports Participation in 1993.* Mt. Prospect, Illinois: National Sporting Goods Association.

O'Brien, S. and Vertinsky, P. (1991). Unfit survivors: Exercise as a resource for aging women. *The Gerontologist*, 31, 347-357.

Palmore, E. (1979). Predictors of successful aging. *The Gerontologist*, 19, 427-431.

Parker, M.A. (1988). Student volunteers: An endangered species? *Campus Activities Programming*, 20 (8), 49-51.

Phillips, M. (1982). Motivation and expectation in successful volunteerism. *Journal of Voluntary Action Research*, 11, 118-125.

Redfering, David and Biasco, Frank. (1982). Volunteering for college credit. *College Student Journal*, 16 (2), 121-123.

Schilke, J.M. (1991). Slowing the aging process with physical activity. *Journal of Gerontological Nursing*, 17 (6), 4-8.

Schor, Juliet B. (1991). *The Overworked American: The Unexpected Decline of Leisure*. Boston, MA: Basic Books.

Shepard, R.J. (1978). *Physical Activity and Aging*. Chicago, Illinois: Croon Helm.

Smith, Everett L. (1981). *Physical Activity: The Foundation of Youth in Aging*. A synopsis of the National Conference on Fitness and Aging, Washington, DC.

Swift, John S., Jr. (1990). Social consciousness and career awareness: emerging link in higher education. *ASHE-ERIC Higher Education Report No. 8*. Washington, DC: Association for the Study of Higher Education.

Tedrick, Ted. (1991). Aging and leisure bibliography. *Activities, Adaptation & Aging*, 15 (4), 87-98.

Reciprocal Volunteering:
Nursing Home Residents
and the Homeless

Ella Denice Hairston

SUMMARY. Nursing home residents and homeless persons (those in transition to independent living) are the beneficiaries of a reciprocal volunteer program. Each of these underserved populations are described as having unmet needs that can be addressed by the other. Selection criterion and a list of possible activities are included in this discussion. *[Article copies available from The Haworth Document Delivery Service: 1-800-342-9678.]*

Many of the factors that precipitate homelessness are not caused by the unique actions of an individual. Society's response would lead one to

Ella Denice Hairston, MS, is affiliated with Ellsworth Associates, Inc., a firm under contract with the Department of Health and Human Services, Head Start Bureau. She is also a consultant with VeJak Research & Managment Services on aging issues.

Address correspondence to the author at: P.O. Box 74, Fieldale, VA 24089.

[Haworth co-indexing entry note]: "Reciprocal Volunteering: Nursing Home Residents and the Homeless," Hairston, Ella Denice. Co-published simultaneously in *Activities, Adaptation & Aging* (The Haworth Press, Inc.) Vol. 20, No. 1, 1995, pp. 91-96; and: *Volunteerism in Geriatric Settings* (ed: Vera R. Jackson), The Haworth Press, Inc., 1995, pp. 91-96. Single or multiple copies of this article/chapter may be purchased from The Haworth Document Delivery Center [1-800-342-9678, 9:00 a.m. - 5:00 p.m. (EST)].

believe that personal pathology or deviance is overwhelmingly the cause of homelessness. However, other precipitating factors, like cataclysmic events, the absense of economic opportunities, and the inequities of public policy, have rendered many homeless.

Society ultimately classifies the homeless population into two groups, the deserving and the undeserving. As a result, some of the homeless are discriminated against in the distribution of resources, thereby receiving less than their needs warrant.

While an inadequate response towards homeless individuals might be easily explained and even widely accepted, one grapples with why another precarious population in our society is also underserved. Like the homeless, many of the elderly are not viewed as contributing members of society, but as individuals who have needs that they can no longer fulfill themselves.

Kimmel (1990) used a measure called the *dependency ratio* to determine the effect of growth of the elderly population on the rest of the population. The dependency ratio calculates the burden of older "dependents" on those people who are economically "productive" (p. 470). Kimmel estimated that before the year 2000 there will be about 19 persons over 65 for every 100 persons between 18 and 64. By the year 2030, this ratio is projected to increase to 29 elderly per 100 persons age 18 to 64 to account for individuals of the postwar baby boom.

In *Kincare and the American Corporation: Solving the Work/Family Dilemma*, Dayle M. Smith (1991) reported that Americans 65 or older numbered 29 million and more than 10,000 Americans were over 100 years old. Projections for the year 2030 indicate that the number of Americans 65 or older will reach 65 million, almost one quarter of the entire population or as many elderly citizens as children (Smith, 1991). America's elderly population is clearly growing at a rapid rate. As the elderly multiply, their needs multiply as well.

UNDERSTANDING NEEDS

Both the homeless and the elderly experience major life issues that impact their abilities to meet needs on their own. These needs are described according to Maslow's hierarchy of basic needs (1970):

1. bodily needs
2. safety and security
3. love, affection, and belongingness
4. self-esteem and esteem of others
5. self-actualization

Homelessness has a direct impact on the two lower levels of need simply because of the nature of the homeless existence. It is often difficult to find adequate shelter, food, or clothing, and many homeless people often live in the streets and shelters where safety and security from physical or emotional harm are constantly in jeopardy (Eddowes & Hranitz, 1989). Since needs are a hierarchy, the three remaining levels of need are indirectly impacted because of a homeless person's difficulty meeting the lower level needs.

The elderly often find it difficult to meet some of their basic needs because skills and faculties have decreased as a result of aging. Declining physical strength and agility make daily activities less manageable or too time consuming. Participation in leisure or recreational activities may even subside not because the desire has left, but because carrying out these activities is too physically demanding.

In some cases, geriatric residents and homeless persons have been uprooted from environments that were comfortable–let alone home to them. Home is generally thought to be a "place of one's dwelling or nurturing with feelings naturally attached to and associated with it."

Homeless persons living in shelters and geriatric nursing home residents are confronted with separation from that place that anchored and helped to define them. Sometimes this separation erodes self-esteem and affects the quality of social, psychological, institutional, and material supports received. The ill effects of this separation may net some degree of detachment from life itself.

Upon further comparison, one concludes that both geriatric nursing home residents and the homeless are unable to function completely independently due to their domicile. In general, both groups desire the highest semblance of independence, but circumstances impede this desire.

THE RECIPROCAL PLAN

This innovative approach seeks to provide geriatric nursing home residents and homeless persons with opportunities for creatively meeting unmet needs through volunteerism. The activity director plays a major role in the identification of nursing home residents capable of participating in this program. The activity director, in cooperation with a social services liaison in the community, is also responsible for the screening and selection of homeless persons nearing transition from shelter to independent living for prospective program inclusion.

Nursing home residents could be engaged in short-term volunteer activities that are appropriate to their abilities, interests, and consistent with the facility's policies. Likewise, homeless volunteers could participate in short-term activities after satisfying health, safety, and welfare guidelines established by the facility.

The success of this program is contingent upon careful screening of volunteers. Hence, it is important that only those homeless persons nearing transition from shelter to independent living be recruited as volunteers. As a part of the transition phase of the homeless person's life, they should be employed (either full-time or part-time) or have a pending commitment for such employment. Homeless volunteers must receive an assessment of skills, abilities, and interests so that they can be adequately matched with an assignment.

The following suggestions are offered as activities for both resident volunteers and homeless volunteers.

Resident Volunteers

Gift-making. Due to a lack of resources, homeless families may not be able to afford gifts for special occasions. Resident volunteers can make birthday and holiday presents for homeless children and families. Gifts made could include blankets, pottery, scarfs, hats, gloves, dolls or stuffed animals for children, or arts and crafts items.

Clothing. Resident volunteers can mend clothing donated to the homeless by area churches or other groups. After the clothing has been recycled it can be denoted to a local shelter.

Grandparenting. Homeless children could benefit from a nursing home visit to "adoptive grandparents." This relationship with the children could provide stability and intergenerational interaction for many who need it. In exchange, the children will serve as a source of emotional fulfillment to residents (Kimmel, 1990).

Written encouragement. Many homeless people go through bouts of depression and despair when faced with the daily demands and outlook of their futures. For these reasons, words of wisdom and encouragement are critically needed to cope during this very difficult time. Resident volunteers can write letters or make cards to encourage a homeless family. Supportive messages may do a world of good.

Homeless Volunteers

Companionship. One of the common feelings that nursing home residents report is isolation. Homeless volunteers of varying ages can become companions to residents. The companion relationship could consist of time spent talking together, work on a special arts or crafts project or an escort to nursing home activities.

Recreation. Volunteers can lead bingo games, aid with sing-a-longs, conduct fitness/exercise sessions, or even coordinate a mini-talent show or performance for residents. With some imagination, the activities could become endless.

Gift making and letter writing. Homeless volunteers could participate in the host of activities listed previously under the heading for resident volunteers. The benefits will be the same. Lives will be enriched and recognition and encouragement offered.

CONCLUSION

Activities that integrate needs and service delivery efforts are worth considering. Our ability to make the best use of our human resources during a time of declining volunteer strength depends on our ability to take risks and to be creative. Reciprocal volunteering offers an atypical approach to enabling two underserved populations to fulfill a few of the basic needs of each other despite societal perceptions that each has very little to offer.

AUTHOR NOTE

Ella Denice Hairston received her Bachelor of Science degree in Family Studies and Master of Science degree in Program Management for Family and Community Development from the College of Human Ecology at the University of Maryland at College Park (UMCP). While at the UMCP, Ms. Hairston structured a program for homeless children residing at a family shelter and volunteered at a university sponsored senior citizen's program. Her graduate thesis entailed a comparison of the depression levels of homeless mothers and low-income mothers with a child in Head Start.

Ms. Ella Denice Hairston, formerly employed with three United Way organizations (Delaware, Maryland, and the District of Columbia-National Capital Area) had oversight and monitoring responsibilities for programs and services offered to homeless persons and the elderly in these jurisdictions. Ms. Hairston also coordinated staff volunteer activities at area nursing homes.

REFERENCES

Eddowes, E.A., & Hranitz, J.R. (1989). Educating children of the homeless. *Childhood Education,* 197-200.

Garrett, G.R., & Schutt, R.K. (1987). The homeless alcoholic, past and present. In *Homelessness: Critical issues for policy and practice* (pp. 29-32). Boston: Boston Foundation.

Kimmel, D.C. (1990). *Adulthood and Aging* (3rd ed.). New York: John Wiley & Sons.

Maslow, A. (1970). *Motivation and personality* (2nd ed.). New York: Harper & Row.

National Coalition for the Homeless. (1988). Homelessness in the United States: Background and federal response. Washington, DC: The Coalition.

National Coalition for the Homeless. (1989). American nightmare: A decade of homelessness in the United States. Washington, DC: The Coalition.

Rivlin, L.G., & Manzo, L.C. (1988). Homeless children in New York City: A view from the 19th century. *Children's Environments Quarterly, 5*(1), 26-33.

Ropers, R.H. (1988). *The invisible homeless: A new urban ecology.* New York: Human Sciences Press.

Smith, D.M. (1991). To grandmother's house we go: Caring for elders. In *Kincare and the American corporation: Solving the work/family dilemma* (pp. 82-97). Homewood, IL: Richard Irwin.

Stark, L. (1987). Blame the system, not its victims. In *Homelessness: Critical issues for policy and practice* (pp. 7-11). Boston: Boston Foundation.

CONCLUDING REMARKS

Keys to a Successful Volunteer Program

Vera R. Jackson

This concluding section offers a compilation of recommendations for successful geriatric volunteer program management based on the content of previous chapters. These recommendations are the keys to enhancing the quality and effectiveness of volunteer programs while addressing the varied needs of volunteers, residents, and the geriatric setting.

RECOMMENDATIONS

1. **Invest in the financial adequacy of your geriatric volunteer program.**
   Assure that funding is available by realistically assessing financial needs. If resources are limited, seek out "aging project" or "aging events" donations from external groups.
2. **Promote your geriatric volunteer program as being cost-effective.**
   Estimate the cumulative dollar value of the time donated and weigh this quantity against expenses incurred. Make sure that senior management and co-workers are aware of the cost savings and benefits to the residents.
3. **Recruit a heterogeneous volunteer pool.**
   Facilitating the participation of disparate demographic groups will promote effective performance and will address equity volunteer issues within the geriatric setting.
4. **Train your volunteers.** Training and orientation will equip your volunteers with job skills and will acquaint them with aging issues, information on how to work with the aged, the geriatric facility's

---

[Haworth co-indexing entry note]: "Keys to a Successful Volunteer Program,"Jackson, Vera R. Co-published simultaneously in *Activities, Adaptation & Aging* (The Haworth Press, Inc.) Vol. 20, No. 1, 1995, pp. 99-101; and: *Volunteerism in Geriatric Settings* (ed: Vera R. Jackson), The Haworth Press, Inc., 1995, pp. 99-101. Single or multiple copies of this article/chapter may be purchased from The Haworth Document Delivery Center [1-800-342-9678, 9:00 a.m. - 5:00 p.m. (EST)].

99

norms, philosophy, and goals. Establish a regular supervisory session for volunteers so that you may gauge the need for additional training and also determine their comfort level with their assignment. Offer in-service training to volunteers regularly. Learning should be a very important element of your volunteer program.

5. **Know thy volunteer.**

Getting to know your volunteer can be accomplished through regular supervisory sessions and during observation times. Determine your volunteers' motivation for wanting to work with your geriatric population and help them to grow through their experiences. Remember to match volunteer abilities with residents' needs.

6. **Let volunteers be managers too.**

Engaging volunteers in the planning and implementation of the geriatric program builds a sense of partnership and will result in renewed commitment and motivation.

7. **Make volunteering fun and/or satisfying.**

Volunteers gain satisfaction and fulfillment from the service they perform. Give geriatric residents occasions to say "thank you" to volunteers. It's up to you to make sure that these opportunities exist.

8. **Evaluate the volunteer program.**

Encourage feedback from volunteers, residents, and other interested parties on aging projects and the overall volunteer program. Implement suggestions that can enhance your program. Annually update program policies and procedures.

9. **Evaluate your volunteers.**

Volunteers need to know that their work is valuable and that they can receive feedback on their performance. Develop a specific volunteer evaluation tool or modify an existing tool used for paid staff. Establish a time for annual evaluations and stick to it.

10. **Be creative in your planning.**

Consider new and different ways of offering activities. Find ways of letting your geriatric residents volunteer for short-term projects. Make learning a two-way street for both volunteers and geriatric residents.

11. **Make recognition a priority.**

Appreciation for service rendered can be accomplished through a number of methods. Ask your volunteers to brain storm a list of informal and formal recognition ideas. Randomly select at least two informal and one formal activities from the list annually. Be sure to give volunteers credit for offering the ideas selected. Continue to solicit ideas and make reasonable attempts to give each idea at least one try.

12. **Remember to take care of "you."**

Seek motivation and professional development from volunteer

association memberships, aging training sessions and seminars, meetings with your peers, and publications designed to enhance geriatric volunteer program management. Find a "mentor" or "colleague" with whom you can share successes, as well as frustrations. Seek out support for your volunteer program from senior management and external aging groups. Don't be afraid to promote the successes of your volunteer program and your hard work.

Index

Haworth
DOCUMENT DELIVERY
SERVICE

This valuable service provides a single-article order form for any article from a Haworth journal.

- *Time Saving:* No running around from library to library to find a specific article.
- *Cost Effective:* All costs are kept down to a minimum.
- *Fast Delivery:* Choose from several options, including same-day FAX.
- *No Copyright Hassles:* You will be supplied by the original publisher.
- *Easy Payment:* Choose from several easy payment methods.

Open Accounts Welcome for ...
- Library Interlibrary Loan Departments
- Library Network/Consortia Wishing to Provide Single-Article Services
- Indexing/Abstracting Services with Single Article Provision Services
- Document Provision Brokers and Freelance Information Service Providers

---

MAIL or *FAX* THIS ENTIRE ORDER FORM TO:

Haworth Document Delivery Service The Haworth Press, Inc. 10 Alice Street Binghamton, NY 13904-1580	**or FAX:** 1-800-895-0582 **or CALL:** 1-800-342-9678 9am-5pm EST

PLEASE SEND ME PHOTOCOPIES OF THE FOLLOWING SINGLE ARTICLES:

1) Journal Title: _____

    Vol/Issue/Year: _____ Starting & Ending Pages: _____

Article Title: _____

2) Journal Title: _____

    Vol/Issue/Year: _____ Starting & Ending Pages: _____

Article Title: _____

3) Journal Title: _____

    Vol/Issue/Year: _____ Starting & Ending Pages: _____

Article Title: _____

4) Journal Title: _____

    Vol/Issue/Year: _____ Starting & Ending Pages: _____

Article Title: _____

(See other side for Costs and Payment Information)

COSTS: Please figure your cost to order quality copies of an article.

1. Set-up charge per article: $8.00
   ($8.00 × number of separate articles) _____

2. Photocopying charge for each article:
   1-10 pages: $1.00 _____

   11-19 pages: $3.00 _____

   20-29 pages: $5.00 _____

   30+ pages: $2.00/10 pages _____

3. Flexicover (optional): $2.00/article _____

4. Postage & Handling: US: $1.00 for the first article/
   $.50 each additional article _____

   Federal Express: $25.00 _____

   Outside US: $2.00 for first article/
   $.50 each additional article _____

5. Same-day FAX service: $.35 per page _____

   GRAND TOTAL: _____

METHOD OF PAYMENT: (please check one)

❑ Check enclosed   ❑ Please ship and bill. PO # _____
(sorry we can ship and bill to bookstores only! All others must pre-pay)

❑ Charge to my credit card: ❑ Visa; ❑ MasterCard; ❑ Discover;
❑ American Express;

Account Number:_____ Expiration date:_____

Signature: *X*_____

Name: _____ Institution: _____

Address: _____

_____

City: _____ State:_____ Zip:_____

Phone Number: _____ FAX Number: _____

MAIL or *FAX* THIS ENTIRE ORDER FORM TO:

Haworth Document Delivery Service	**or FAX:** 1-800-895-0582
The Haworth Press, Inc.	**or CALL:** 1-800-342-9678
10 Alice Street	9am-5pm EST)
Binghamton, NY 13904-1580	

For Product Safety Concerns and Information please contact our EU
representative GPSR@taylorandfrancis.com Taylor & Francis Verlag GmbH,
Kaufingerstraße 24, 80331 München, Germany

Batch number: 08153776

Printed by Printforce, the Netherlands